The Light That Refuses to Stay Out

A Meditation on Conscience, Power, and Human Nature

EVAN HOPE

Good Heart. Open Mind. Coexist.

© 2026 Evan Hope. All rights reserved.
No part of this publication may be reproduced, distributed, or transmitted in any form or by any means without the prior written permission of the author.
Author: Evan Hope
Published 2026, Australia
Good Heart. Open Mind. Coexist.

Contents

A Note Before We Begin

This is not an academic book.

It does not footnote every claim or situate itself neatly within scholarly debate. There are better books for that — written by people with far more patience for the machinery of formal argument than I possess.

Nor is this an attack on religion.

Some of the greatest moral courage I have witnessed in my life came from people whose faith was the source of it. If anything, this book is written out of respect for what the great traditions were trying to reach at their best — and out of grief for the distance that sometimes exists between those original moral impulses and the institutions that later grew around them.

This is not a political manifesto either. It does not belong to a party, an ideology, or a movement. The reflections that follow apply the same scrutiny to the left and the right, to religious and secular institutions, to democracies and dictatorships alike. Because the pattern this book is tracing does not belong to any one system.

It belongs to human beings.

At its core, this book is a personal reflection on conscience — on the strange moral sensitivity human beings seem to carry long before any doctrine, nation, or institution teaches them what to believe. It is about the forces that deepen that sensitivity, and the forces that slowly silence it: fear, power, tribalism, comfort, ideology, survival.

It is also about history. About what repeatedly happens when human beings stop examining the systems they inherit and begin confusing obedience with morality. And about what it might mean, from whatever position we occupy in life, to resist that drift toward silence.

I am a doctor who grew up in Myanmar and now lives in Australia. I have seen what happens when institutions built to protect human dignity are captured by the very people entrusted to defend it.

I have also carried the quieter burden familiar to many who leave troubled countries behind — the guilt of the person who escaped while others stayed.

I am not a philosopher, historian, or theologian. I am simply someone who has spent years unable to stop thinking about these questions. This book is the result of that thinking: imperfect, unfinished, and offered not as a conclusion, but as an invitation.

Read it with whatever you believe.

Bring your faith, if you have it. Bring your scepticism, if you do not. Bring your politics, your history, your wounds, your doubts, and your own experience of what it feels like when conscience is honoured — and when it is overridden.

This book asks questions more often than it answers them. That is deliberate. The questions that matter most are rarely the ones another person can answer for us completely. Each of us must confront them from where we stand, with the life we have lived and the limits of what we know.

And I may be wrong about parts of this — or indeed all of it.

What follows is simply how the world appears from where I stand: from one particular life shaped by one particular history, with its losses, compromises, fears, escapes, and contradictions. Someone standing elsewhere will inevitably see things I cannot. That is not a weakness of honest thinking. It is its condition.

This is not an optimistic book in the simple sense. But neither is it hopeless.

The hope it offers is not the comfort that comes from looking away. It is the quieter and more difficult kind that becomes possible only after we have looked directly at what is broken and refused to pretend otherwise.

False comfort closes the eyes.

Honest hope keeps them open.

That is all this book is trying to do.

To keep them open long enough that the reader can no longer look at the world in quite the same way again.

CHAPTER ONE

God Is Dead

In 1882, the philosopher Friedrich Nietzsche wrote words that have unsettled people ever since. God is dead. We have killed him. Most who read them assumed he was celebrating. He was not. One widely held reading of Nietzsche is that he was sounding an alarm — that his concern was not theological but moral.

That the ideas holding civilisation together — human dignity, the obligation to care for the weak, the sense that some things are simply wrong regardless of who benefits — had always drawn their authority from a source that was disappearing. And nobody seemed to notice.

That is what Nietzsche meant. And it is worth taking seriously.

This book begins from a quieter place. Not a philosophical argument. Just an observation — one that has stayed with me across years of thinking about faith, about history, about the country I was born in and the one I came to.

The damage done in God's name across history was not done primarily by the people who stopped believing. It was done, in the main, by the faithful — by people who prayed, who observed every ritual, who were completely certain they were on the right side — and who never stopped to ask what the teaching they carried actually required of them.

Perhaps that begins to look less like faith in its original sense, and more like belief that has stopped listening to itself. Through faith inherited rather than chosen. Through the slow replacement of a living moral engagement with the comfort of belonging to something that once meant more than it does now.

I offer this not as a correction of Nietzsche. Only as a thought that kept returning. That the shell of religion, emptied of its original meaning, can be as dangerous as no religion at all. Because the shell often still carries the authority — and perhaps for that reason is harder to question than straightforward disbelief.

It still speaks in God's name. And history suggests, again and again, what happens when that authority is no longer answerable to the conscience it was built to serve.

One thing this book is not. It is not an argument that religion is the source of the world's moral failures. The chapters that follow use religious history as their first extended example because religion is where human beings made their earliest and most sustained attempts to institutionalise moral life at scale — and therefore where the pattern of that institutionalisation and its corruption is most thoroughly documented.

The same logic operates in secular political systems, in the machinery of empire, in the calculations of great powers who have decided that the suffering of small nations is an acceptable cost. This is not a failure specific to faith. It is a failure of human nature.

* * *

Belief Without Understanding

What I kept noticing, the more I read and the more I watched, was this: some of the greatest damage done in God's name came not from disbelief but from certainty that went unexamined. By people who attended their services, recited their prayers, followed their rituals, and were completely certain they were on the right side — while conducting wars, justifying slavery, oppressing women, and persecuting anyone who looked or thought or loved differently.

How does that happen?

It begins when belief becomes habit. When faith becomes something absorbed rather than chosen. When the question of what this actually means stops being asked. Somewhere in that process, what remains is the shell — the building, the ritual, the identity, the language — but hollowed out. That begins to look less like faith, and more like obedience without understanding.

Some would argue the opposite — that religion has been the primary source of moral behaviour, not its corruptor. That without the church, the mosque, the temple, the conscience itself would have no language to speak in.

That argument deserves attention.

And there is truth in it. At their best, religious traditions have elevated moral behaviour on a scale no individual conscience could achieve alone. They built hospitals, ended empires of cruelty, gave ordinary people a reason to treat strangers with dignity.

That is not the question I am asking. Religion has done good — genuinely, undeniably, on an extraordinary scale. The question I keep returning to is what happens when the institution built to serve the moral purpose begins, slowly and almost invisibly, to serve itself instead.

That is not a condemnation of religion. It is an observation about human beings. We are capable of extraordinary moral clarity. We are equally capable of using the language of that clarity to justify its exact opposite — and believing sincerely that we are doing right while we do it.

If there is a common thread in the worst things done in God's name, it is not cruelty alone. It is the indifference — the failure to ask — that allowed the cruelty to continue beneath the canopy of the sacred.

I am not exempt from this. There are things I was taught to believe before I had the language to question them, and I am still finding out which ones I have actually examined and which ones I have simply carried.

What keeps striking me is that the mechanism is not religious at all. It is human.

Some readers may object that religion is not unique in producing cruelty — and they would be right. The twentieth century alone contains enough secular atrocities to destroy any naïve belief that removing religion removes human brutality. Stalinist purges, Mao's Cultural Revolution, fascist nationalism, racial pseudoscience, and revolutionary terror all emerged from systems that claimed moral certainty without necessarily relying on God.

The pattern is deeper than religion. Human beings construct narratives that divide the world into the righteous and the condemned. Once a system convinces itself that history, God, race, ideology, or even "progress" itself is unquestionably on its side, conscience can slowly become subordinate to the system.

The danger is not faith alone. The danger is certainty without humility, power without accountability, and identity strong enough to silence empathy.

* * *

What the Rules Were Really For

Every religious tradition was born into a specific world — a world of scarce resources, constant violence, high mortality, and communities that could be wiped out by a single bad season or a single hostile neighbour.

They were speaking to communities with immediate, desperate problems. And many of the rules that emerged from those moments were not purely spiritual.

Scholars disagree about the precise origins of religious law, and within traditions these origins are understood very differently. But the historical pattern is suggestive.

Dietary laws that prevented contamination in climates where food spoiled quickly. Rules around marriage and reproduction that ensured a community could replace its dead. Codes of warfare that directed violence outward rather than inward. Prohibitions on behaviours that destabilised the social order when the social order was all that stood between survival and collapse.

These rules worked. That is why they survived. But they survived dressed in the most powerful language available — the language of God. Because most of us tend to obey divine commands in ways we do not obey practical advice. And because the leaders who shaped these traditions understood, whether consciously or not, that a rule framed as God's will is a rule that cannot easily be questioned.

And so today we inherit instructions written for a desert community two thousand years ago and apply them to a world those authors could not have imagined. Not because the wisdom in them has been carefully considered and found still relevant. But because questioning them was never permitted.

The rule outlived its reason. The obedience outlived the understanding. I am not sure what to call that. But I am not sure it is the same thing as faith.

* * *

When Power Wears God's Clothes

But survival was only part of it. The other part is harder to admit.

Alongside the genuine moral teachings of every tradition, there is a second current running through the history of religion. The current of authority. Of control. Of human beings discovering that the language of the sacred is among the most effective tools ever devised for keeping other human beings in line.

A person who obeys because they are afraid will stop the moment the threat disappears. A person who obeys because they believe God requires it will obey in the dark, alone, when no one is watching. That difference is not a small thing to a leader trying to hold a community together. It is everything.

In many traditions, at particular moments in history, rules that confined women were given divine sanction. Hierarchies that placed certain groups at the bottom were codified in sacred law. The questioning of established authority was framed not as intellectual honesty but as spiritual danger — a threat to the whole community, not merely to those who held power.

This did not require cynicism. It rarely does. Most of us are remarkably capable of believing the things that also happen to serve our interests. A leader who has built his life around a tradition genuinely believes he is protecting something sacred. When doubt and dissent weaken the social fabric he feels responsible for, silencing the questioner feels like an act of protection.

He is not lying. He has simply confused the institution with the truth it was built to serve. And once that confusion takes hold, the tradition begins to serve power rather than challenge it.

* * *

The Book Was Written by Human Hands

There is something every scholar of religion knows but few congregations are ever told plainly. The texts we hold as sacred did not fall from the sky fully formed. They were written by human hands, copied by human hands, translated by human hands, selected by human hands, and interpreted by human hands at every step of the journey from their origin to the page you are reading today.

The Bible as it exists was assembled over centuries, with books included and excluded by councils of men who had theological and political interests in the outcome. The Quran was compiled by human editors from oral traditions and written fragments after Muhammad's death. The Torah emerged from multiple sources over hundreds of years. None of this is disputed by serious scholars. Much of it is simply not communicated to the people in the pews.

This is not an argument against faith. It is an argument for honesty about what faith actually rests on. Within their own traditions, these processes of transmission and interpretation are understood very differently — as the working of divine providence through human hands, as the preservation of revelation across time, as the living tradition of a community.

Some will say that acknowledging human involvement in sacred texts is not threatening to faith at all — that God works through human hands, and that the imperfection of the vessel does not diminish the truth carried inside it.

But it still leaves the question open. If human hands shaped the text, and human hands have interests, then some discernment is required. Which parts carry the original moral truth? And which parts carry the fingerprints of the moment, the community, and the people who decided what stayed and what was quietly removed?

That instruction — do not question, do not distinguish, treat every word as equally and absolutely binding — is itself one of the most consequential additions any authority ever made to a religious tradition. It takes the genuine moral wisdom inside the text and locks it in place alongside everything else, making it difficult to separate the living thing from the material that was always only human.

The same Bible was used to justify slavery and to abolish it. The same Quranic tradition produced scholars who argued for the full intellectual and spiritual equality of women and legal systems that treated women as property.

The text did not change. The interpretation did. And the interpretation always, in some way, served someone.

> *Rigidity is not devotion. It is the abandonment of the very engagement that the tradition requires. The letter of the law without the spirit is not faith preserved. It is faith replaced.*

For the person of genuine faith, none of this is an argument for abandonment. If anything, it is an argument for something more demanding — that faith cannot be fully outsourced. Cannot be handed entirely to an institution, a scholar, a priest, or a text and accepted without the ongoing work of asking: what does this mean, what does it require, does this interpretation still serve the original moral purpose or has it begun serving something else?

Keep the faith. Question the interpretation. And never stop asking what the teaching was actually for.

Because at the beginning of every tradition, beneath everything that was later added, there was a person pointing at something already present in every human being — a conscience, a moral instinct, a knowledge of right and wrong that existed before any doctrine arrived to name it.

If the original moral instinct preceded every religion that tried to codify it, then a question becomes unavoidable: where did that instinct come from? And why does it keep appearing — stubbornly, consistently — even when every institution built to honour it has failed?

CHAPTER TWO

Before the First Word

I keep returning to the same question.

Not as a philosopher. Not as a theologian. Simply as a person trying to understand what human beings are before the world finishes shaping them — what it is we arrive with.

Because long before children understand religion, politics, law, nationalism, or ideology, something already seems present.

A child sees another child crying and becomes distressed themselves. Someone witnesses humiliation and feels something recoil internally before forming an argument about it. A stranger rushes toward danger to help another stranger before calculation fully catches up.

Something responds before doctrine arrives.

* * *

Before We Learn the World

The older I become, the harder it is to believe human beings begin as empty moral space waiting for systems to write themselves onto us completely.

The systems shape what is already present rather than creating morality from nothing.

I do not mean human beings are naturally pure. History clearly argues against that fantasy.

Children can also be selfish, territorial, cruel, possessive, jealous, and impulsive very early in life. Anyone who has watched children closely knows this too.

Many researchers in developmental psychology observe something appearing in infants before significant cultural conditioning — a sensitivity to fairness, a distress at witnessing harm, a recognition of the other as real. The debate about what is truly innate and what is absorbed very early continues. But something seems to be present before doctrine arrives to name it.

* * *

The First Silence

I think many people remember, if they are honest, moments from childhood where conscience appeared before explanation.

A moment where something felt wrong long before we possessed the language to defend why.

Watching another child excluded. Hearing cruelty in an adult's voice. Seeing fear in someone's face. The reaction comes first.

Then slowly the world teaches us when to suppress it. Not always maliciously. Sometimes through survival. Sometimes through culture. Sometimes through exhaustion. Sometimes through belonging.

A child may instinctively protest unfairness until they learn that questioning authority carries consequences. Another learns that vulnerability invites humiliation. Another learns that silence keeps the household stable.

Over time, conscience does not necessarily disappear. It becomes negotiated.

* * *

The Two Pulls

Every human being seems to carry two opposing pulls simultaneously.

One moves toward empathy, connection, compassion, fairness, truth, and recognition of another person's humanity.

The other moves toward fear, tribalism, self-protection, domination, resentment, and indifference.

I know both sides of this from the inside. I have felt the pull toward genuine care and the pull toward self-interest and I am under no illusion about which one wins without effort.

The line separating cruelty from kindness does not run cleanly between good people and bad people. It runs through individual human beings, through families, through institutions, through nations, through entire civilisations.

That is why history repeats itself so often. Human beings keep imagining evil belongs primarily to other kinds of people. And then ordinary people, under fear or ideology or humiliation or power, become capable of things they once believed unimaginable.

There are people for whom the pull toward others is strong and natural — people for whom empathy is not an effort but a default. They are not saints. They still have the other capacity inside them. But their default is toward care, and circumstances have to work hard against that.

And there are people for whom the pull runs the other way. Not broken by circumstance alone, but oriented differently from early on. Some people seem more vulnerable to certain destructive tendencies than others, even when raised in similar conditions. Why that is remains genuinely uncertain. Pretending it is never the case does not protect anyone. It only makes us slower to recognise when it is.

Most people spend their lives somewhere in the middle — capable of genuine generosity and genuine selfishness. Pulled toward their better nature by love and suffering and example. Pulled away from it by fear and self-interest and the comfort of not having to think too hard. The vast middle of humanity, navigating the dial with varying degrees of success.

That navigation is what morality actually is. Not the following of a list of rules. Not the performance of correct opinions. But the ongoing, imperfect, daily attempt to let the reality of other people matter.

* * *

Fear Changes Morality

Fear may be one of the strongest forces acting on conscience.

A frightened person thinks differently from a safe one. Fear narrows attention. It prioritises survival. It reduces complexity. It makes tribal thinking emotionally attractive because groups feel safer than uncertainty.

Under enough fear, people begin asking what protects me before they ask what is right.

I do not say this from superiority. I grew up in a country where fear shaped ordinary life quietly. Conversations lowered when strangers entered rooms. Political caution became instinctive. Silence became part of the emotional architecture of survival.

Fear changes people. Not always dramatically. Often gradually enough that they barely notice themselves adapting.

* * *

Comfort Does It Too

But fear is not the only thing capable of weakening conscience.

Comfort can do it as well. A comfortable person can slowly become insulated from the suffering sustaining their stability. Entire societies can.

Not because people become evil. Because distance weakens emotional immediacy. The suffering happens elsewhere. To other people. Through systems complicated enough that responsibility feels abstract.

Sometimes I think indifference in wealthy societies is less a deliberate moral failure than a form of emotional exhaustion mixed with distance.

But the outcome can still become dangerous. The person who looks away out of fear and the person who looks away out of comfort are not morally identical. Yet both kinds of silence still allow harmful systems to continue functioning.

* * *

What Suffering Teaches

There is one experience that has more power than almost any other to move the dial toward genuine moral seriousness.

Suffering.

Not suffering in the abstract. Suffering that is felt, faced, and processed honestly rather than buried or redirected outward into blame.

A felt understanding of what it means to be vulnerable. A recognition that the person in pain in front of you is as real as you are.

This is why the greatest moral teachers across history were almost never people who had lived comfortable and untested lives. They had been through something. And what they brought back from that was not bitterness but a more vivid understanding of what it means to be human.

Suffering can also do the opposite. A person who is hurt and does not process it, who turns the pain into grievance and the grievance into ideology, can become someone whose conscience has been overwhelmed rather than deepened.

Both outcomes are possible from the same experience. Suffering alone does not determine the moral outcome. What matters is what happens to the suffering afterward — whether it opens the person toward others or closes them down.

* * *

When the Soil Is Poisoned

But the seed requires conditions.

A child born into a community where cruelty is normalised, where trauma accumulates across generations without being named or processed, where survival has required the suppression of empathy — that child is not born without moral instinct.

But it is buried under the weight of what survival required.

The capacity for empathy that research shows is present from the earliest months of life can be overlaid by years of conditioning so thorough that the original instinct becomes inaccessible without enormous effort.

And then something else happens. The mind that survived the forming period does not simply carry the wound. It builds a framework around the wound that makes the wound feel like wisdom.

So the wound becomes a worldview.

The harm received becomes evidence of how the world works. The harm given becomes evidence of strength, of cultural necessity, of survival logic. The indifference of others becomes proof that care is weakness. The cruelty of authority becomes the model for what power looks like.

The entitlement arrives last. The quiet certainty that the harm is not only acceptable but deserved. That the target had it coming. That this is simply how things are.

This is not evil in the dramatic sense. It is the ordinary operation of a human mind that was shaped by specific conditions and then protected itself by turning those conditions into a philosophy.

Understanding this does not excuse the harm. It explains the mechanism. The question of what it would take to interrupt it — that remains open.

* * *

The Fragile Thing

I do not think conscience is infinitely strong.

Human beings can absolutely become desensitised. Entire societies can. Propaganda works. Fear works. Tribalism works. Power works. Comfort works. History proves this repeatedly.

And yet history also shows something else.

Again and again, even inside deeply corrupted systems, some people still resist. Quietly sometimes. Imperfectly. At enormous cost. A person tells the truth anyway. A stranger protects someone vulnerable anyway. A citizen refuses participation anyway.

The system does not fully erase the conscience. It fights constantly to overpower it.

The moral instinct — the conscience, the capacity to recognise dignity and cruelty for what they are — is present as a starting point. Everything else — every religion, every legal system, every political philosophy, every tradition of moral reasoning — was built on top of it. Sometimes honouring it. Sometimes obscuring it. Sometimes using the language of conscience to justify its opposite.

Which means that when we evaluate those systems we already have a standard available. Not a perfect standard. Not a complete one. But one that precedes every system that has ever tried to claim it.

Those questions do not require a degree to ask. They require only the willingness to take seriously what you already sense — that some things cause real harm, that some things honour real dignity, and that the difference matters.

Perhaps civilisation depends largely on whether enough people keep that fragile thing alive in one another long enough for the next generation to inherit it too.

CHAPTER THREE

What Blindness Permits

History is not subtle about this. It left the evidence everywhere, in plain sight, for anyone willing to look honestly. What follows are not isolated incidents or the behaviour of a few bad actors. They are recurring outcomes — and once you see them clearly, they are difficult to unsee.

The civil rights leaders who faced down violence did so singing hymns.

History holds both. What follows is not a verdict on religion. It is a study of what happens when a specific pattern takes hold.

* * *

Done in God's Name

Killing people of a different faith, declared not merely permitted but holy. The rape of women from conquered communities, treated as a right of victory. Breeding as a strategy — populate, assimilate, outnumber, until another culture simply disappears beneath yours.

These things were not done by people who thought they were doing wrong. They were done by people who had stopped asking whether they were doing right — and found, in that silence, a permission they had not examined. A survival calculation. A fear. A need for power dressed in sacred language because sacred language was the most powerful tool available.

That does not make any of it right. It makes it human. And that is almost more disturbing. Because it means these things did not come from religion. They came from us. Religion was simply the vehicle we used to make them feel authorised.

* * *

When Institutions Become Self-Protective

Every institution faces the same temptation eventually — to preserve itself first.

Religious institutions are not unique in this. Governments do it. Political parties do it. Corporations and media organisations and revolutions do it once they become states. Over time, survival quietly replaces purpose.

The institution still speaks the language of morality, justice, truth, or compassion. But increasingly its energy goes toward maintaining authority, suppressing threats, and protecting structure. Not always consciously. Often sincerely. Most people inside institutions do not believe they are acting corruptly. They believe they are defending something valuable from chaos and attack.

The danger emerges when protecting the institution becomes morally indistinguishable from protecting truth itself. At that point, criticism becomes betrayal. Questioning becomes danger. Conscience becomes subordinate to loyalty.

* * *

The Human Need for Certainty

One of the most difficult things for human beings to tolerate is genuine uncertainty.

We want stable answers. Clear identities. A framework that tells us who we are, where we belong, and which side of history we stand on. Religious systems provided that stability for centuries. So did nations, political ideologies, and revolutionary movements. The structure matters less than the psychological function.

Belonging reduces fear. Certainty reduces anxiety. Shared identity reduces loneliness. That is why inherited systems become emotionally powerful long before they become intellectually examined.

Questioning them feels destabilising not merely because beliefs are challenged, but because identity itself becomes uncertain. If the framework collapses, what remains? That fear — often unspoken — helps sustain institutions long after their contradictions become visible. It explains why people sometimes defend systems that demonstrably harm others. The defence is not always rational calculation. Sometimes it is existential protection.

* * *

The Difference Between Faith and Submission

Faith is not the same as submission.

A living faith wrestles, questions, reflects, and returns repeatedly to conscience and moral purpose. Submission avoids the struggle entirely. It replaces engagement with obedience, complexity with certainty, reflection with inherited answers.

Institutions often prefer submission because submission is stable. But moral growth rarely emerges from stability alone.

The people who transformed religious traditions from within — the reformers, the abolitionists, the moral visionaries — were almost always individuals willing to question prevailing interpretations while remaining committed to the ethical core beneath them. They were not rejecting faith. They were rescuing it from the institution surrounding it.

This chapter is not an argument against religion. It is an argument for the kind of faith that keeps examining itself — that stays in contact with the conscience underneath the doctrine rather than mistaking the doctrine for the conscience.

These examples feel distant. Distance makes it easier. The harder question is what the same logic looks like when the distance collapses — when the justification is not historical but present.

* * *

When the Past Speaks Into the Present

Consider what happened not in the distant past but in recent memory. A religious leader, speaking publicly, declared that girls as young as thirteen are fit for marriage and called on his followers to live by religious law that permits it.

Now ask the honest question. Who is right?

The religious leader would say God is right, and God's law does not expire with changing fashion. The modern state would say the law is right, and the law exists to protect children from harm they cannot consent to.

It came from a world in which life expectancy was thirty years. In which a girl who was not married by her mid-teens might never be married at all. In which the concept of childhood as a protected stage of development did not exist, because survival did not permit it.

The vast majority of believers in most traditions do not hold or act on such interpretations. But where they do occur, the person insisting on them is not protecting a sacred tradition so much as protecting a specific interpretation — one shaped by a world that is gone — and calling it divine so that it cannot be questioned.

* * *

What Remains

I grew up inside a tradition shaped by this history. Not the crusades or the Mongols — those are not my history. But the Buddhism that was bent into a tool of submission. The faith that was genuine at its root and used for purposes its origin could not have sanctioned. So I am not writing this from the outside. I am writing it from inside the question.

So this is what it can mean to kill God.

Not the dramatic act of a civilisation losing its faith. Something quieter and more persistent. The slow replacement of understanding with performance. Of genuine moral engagement with the comfort of compliance. Of a living question with a dead answer inherited from someone else and never examined.

And yet. Through all of it — through the conquests and the corruptions, the rules written for survival, the texts shaped by human hands, the interpretations bent toward power — something at the original center of every tradition remains worth honouring.

Go back far enough in any tradition and you find the same thing — a person, or a moment, oriented entirely toward one question. What do we owe one another? Not how to build an empire. Not how to maintain a hierarchy. Simply that.

To honour religion genuinely is not to follow every rule without question. It is to stay in contact with that original question. To hold every interpretation up against the conscience — the same moral sensitivity that was there before the first word was written — and to have the honesty to say when the answer does not match.

Honor the faith. Examine the interpretation. Keep asking what it was for.

Because the religions of the world did not give us our moral instinct. They inherited it. At their best they deepened and extended it in ways that individual conscience alone could not achieve. The task is learning to tell the difference between when they are doing that — and when they are doing something else entirely.

I say this knowing it is easier to write than to live. Examining what you were given requires a courage that the institution was specifically designed to make unnecessary. I have not always had that courage either.

CHAPTER FOUR

The Accident of Birth

Nobody chooses where they are born.

That single fact — so obvious it barely seems worth stating — may be the most important thing to understand about why human beings believe what they believe. The child born in Kabul in 1990 did not choose Islam.

The child born in Bangkok did not choose Buddhism.

The child born in rural Alabama did not choose evangelical Christianity. The child born in Mumbai did not choose Hinduism. They were handed a complete world — a language, a set of values, a moral framework, a relationship with the divine, an understanding of what is right and what is wrong — before they were old enough to question any of it. The framework you are born into does not feel like a choice. It feels like reality itself.

* * *

The World Already Assembled

Think about what it means to arrive in a world already assembled.

Before you could walk, before you had words for any of it, the answers were already being installed. Not through instruction — children cannot receive instruction before they have language. Through atmosphere.

Through the texture of daily life. Through what the adults around you treated as obvious and what they treated as unthinkable. Through the rituals performed without explanation because they needed no explanation.

By the time you were old enough to ask why, you already knew the answers. You had absorbed them the way you absorbed your mother tongue — not by studying it but by living inside it until it became the only language you knew how to think in. And the remarkable thing is that you did not choose any of it — and yet it feels more like you than anything you will ever consciously decide.

This is not unique to any tradition. It is the universal human experience. The child raised inside strict religious observance and the child raised in a secular household with no religion at all are both receiving a complete world before they can evaluate it. Both are being shaped. The only difference is by what.

And the shaping goes deeper than belief. It goes all the way down to the instincts. To what feels natural and what feels wrong. To which kinds of people seem trustworthy and which seem threatening. These are not opinions formed by reasoning. They are orientations formed by immersion. They feel, to most of us who carry them, less like conclusions and more like perception itself.

* * *

The Certainty That Proves Nothing

This dismantles one of the most persistent and damaging ideas in the history of religion — the idea that people who believe differently are choosing wrongly.

That the Muslim who has never seriously encountered Christianity is somehow rejecting it. That the Buddhist who was never exposed to the Quran is turning away from truth. In most cases none of that is true. They are not making a choice. They are living inside the one that was made for them. And so, in exactly the same way, are you.

Some will push back here. People do convert. People do leave the tradition they were born into and adopt another — sometimes at great personal cost. That is real and it matters. Anyone who examines their inherited faith and chooses it consciously is in a different relationship to it than someone who simply absorbed it and never looked.

But they are the exception, not the rule. And even the person who converts is converting to something — usually a tradition they encountered through the accident of which community they moved into, which person they fell in love with, which book they happened to pick up. The framework we end up in is almost always shaped by forces that preceded any deliberate decision we made about it.

Here is what that feels like from the inside. The belief does not feel inherited. It feels discovered. It feels like the conclusion you arrived at through your own honest reckoning with the world. That feeling is real. And it is largely the product of absorption rather than examination.

> *Conviction is not the same as correctness. The confidence with which a belief is held tells you a great deal about how it was formed. It tells you much less about whether it is true.*

* * *

The Second Shaping — Upbringing

But birth is only the first layer. Even within the tradition you were handed, a more intimate and more powerful shaping force is at work.

Your family. Your specific parents, with their specific relationship to the faith they nominally belonged to — devout or indifferent, rigid or questioning, warm or frightened. The neighbourhood and the school and the friends who surrounded you before you had any basis for choosing them. The experiences that accumulated in your earliest years — the kindnesses that taught you the world could be trusted, the cruelties that taught you it could not.

Two people born into the same religion, in the same country, in the same decade, can end up with moral frameworks so different they barely recognise each other as members of the same tradition. Because the religion was the raw material. The upbringing was the sculptor.

And the sculptor works on material that cannot resist being shaped. The child has no defence against the atmosphere they are immersed in. No critical distance from the values being transmitted. No way to say — I will take this part and leave that part.

They receive it whole. They become it. And only much later — if ever — do they develop enough distance to ask what exactly it was they received, and whether it was worth keeping.

A child raised inside a faith by parents who practiced it as a living moral engagement absorbs something very different from a child raised inside the same faith by parents who practiced it as identity and performance. The words are the same. The rituals are the same. The God being named is the same. But what forms in the child is not the same at all.

* * *

What Traditions Provide

Every tradition — religious, philosophical, political — provides something that human beings genuinely need. Story. Ritual. Community gathered around something larger than the individual self. A framework that makes sense of suffering and gives shape to what is owed to others.

This applies to religion. It applies equally to the political ideologies that function as secular faiths — the communist who was raised inside a system that answered every question, the nationalist whose identity was formed by the story of the nation, the free-market economist who absorbed the catechism of incentives and efficiency before they had words to evaluate it. Each inherited a complete framework. Each experienced it as truth rather than as inheritance.

I grew up in a country where Buddhism was the air. Where it shaped everything about how people understood suffering, hierarchy, and what was owed to whom. I did not choose it any more than the child born in Alabama chose evangelical Christianity or the child born in Beijing chose the political framework of the state. We all received our answers before we were old enough to question them.

* * *

What the Accident of Birth Actually Means

Which brings us to the only conclusion that the evidence of history, the reality of human psychology, and the simple fact of how we are born actually supports.

We cannot choose where we enter this world. We cannot choose the tradition we inherit, the language our moral instincts first learn to speak, the community whose assumptions shape us before we are old enough to examine them. The person who holds different beliefs from yours was almost certainly shaped by a different set of circumstances. The same capacity for conviction. Different material to work with.

That recognition does not require you to abandon what you believe. It requires something harder — to hold what you were given alongside the knowledge that someone born elsewhere was given something different, and that the accident of birth is not a theological argument. Not a political argument. Not evidence that your framework is correct and theirs is mistaken.

To look across the divide at the person shaped by different circumstances and see not a person who chose wrong but a person who was shaped differently — that is the most demanding thing the accident of birth asks of us.

Because the destination underneath all the different languages, the different rituals, the different names for what matters — has always been the same question. How should human beings treat one another?

A good heart. The willingness to feel what others feel. To let their reality be as real to you as your own.

An open mind. The willingness to examine what you were given. To ask whether what you inherited honours the moral instinct underneath it or obscures it.

Coexistence. The recognition that the world contains people born into different complete worlds, all of them navigating the same darkness with different lights. And that the darkness does not care which light you are carrying.

A Good Heart. An Open Mind. Coexist.

CHAPTER FIVE

The Only Real Prison

"The only real prison is fear, and the only real freedom is freedom from fear." — Aung San Suu Kyi

She said those words from inside a country that had made fear into policy. A country where the prison was not only literal but also structural. Built into the culture, the education, the religion, the daily texture of life under a system designed to make resistance feel not just dangerous but unthinkable.

She said them after years of house arrest, isolated from her family, watched by soldiers, offered her freedom repeatedly on the condition that she leave and never return. She refused. She stayed. And she kept saying that the only prison was fear.

This chapter is about what that means when you are not Aung San Suu Kyi. When you are someone born into a normal family, trying to survive inside a system built on exactly the fear she was describing.

When the choice is not between heroism and cowardice but between survival and destruction. When the lesson was not taught in a classroom but lived in the body across three generations.

It is also, in part, a personal chapter. Because the ideas in this book did not come from libraries alone. They came from a life. And that life began in Myanmar. If you have never lived under a military dictatorship, what follows may feel distant.

But the mechanism it describes — fear installed so deeply it becomes culture, indifference trained so thoroughly it feels like wisdom — operates wherever power goes unchecked. The names and the flags change. The dynamic does not.

* * *

Three Generations

My great-grandparents came from China. They left during the communist upheaval, carrying nothing except the willingness to start again in a new country. They arrived in Myanmar and did what refugees across history have always done when given even a fraction of a chance — they worked.

They built. They accumulated, slowly and through enormous effort, a life that looked like stability. A factory. A business. A house. The material foundation of a family's future.

Then one day the government took it.

Not through violence, though violence was always the implied alternative. Through policy. The military government of Myanmar, in its drive to consolidate power and assert a particular vision of national identity, turned on the Chinese community.

The businesses were nationalised. The properties were seized. The wealth accumulated across a generation of sacrifice was transferred, by decree, to the state. My family was left with nothing and told to start again.

They did. Because what else do you do? You survive. You rebuild what you can. You learn the lesson the system just taught you — that what you build can be taken, that the law protects those who hold power and no one else, that the safest response to injustice is to keep your head down and stay out of its way.

That lesson did not stay in that generation. It became the atmosphere the next generation breathed. The unspoken understanding transmitted not through words but through the way adults behaved when authority was present, through what topics were never raised at the dinner table, through the instinct — trained so deeply it no longer felt like a choice — to look away from trouble before trouble looked back at you.

* * *

Fear as Architecture

To understand what a military dictatorship does to a society, you have to understand that it does not primarily operate through violence. Violence is expensive. It creates martyrs. It produces the very resistance it is trying to suppress.

What a dictatorship runs on, at its most efficient, is fear. And fear, sustained long enough, reshapes people from the inside. It teaches them to do the work of the system themselves — to self-censor, to look away, to stay quiet, to train their children in the same quietness.

The regime does not need to silence every person. It only needs enough people afraid, often enough, that silence becomes the norm.

In Myanmar, that silence had its own infrastructure. The press was controlled. Education was managed the same way — the history you learned, the values you absorbed, the understanding of your own country filtered through the lens of what the regime needed you to believe.

The result was not a population of people who agreed with the dictatorship. It was a population of people who had learned that disagreement, expressed out loud, in public, was not a risk worth taking.

You could disappear. That was not a metaphor. People did disappear. And that knowledge — carried quietly, never quite spoken — was the real architecture of control. Not the soldiers on the street. The knowledge of what happened to the ones who spoke.

* * *

What Buddhism Became

Buddhism is one of the most genuinely peaceful moral traditions in human history. At its origin it was a radical act of compassion. A man gave up wealth and comfort to sit with the reality of suffering until he understood it. He then spent the rest of his life teaching others that the root of all harm was the illusion of a self more important than the world around it.

The first precept of Buddhist ethics is non-harm. The cultivation of compassion for all beings, without exception, is not an advanced practice in Buddhism. It is the beginning.

I say what follows as someone who grew up Buddhist and who remains so. The tradition I am about to describe is not Buddhism as its founders understood it or as the majority of its practitioners live it.

It is what a particular political power did to Buddhism in one place over a particular period of time. The tradition was used. It was not corrupted at its root. It was distorted at its surface by people who needed it to serve their purposes.

What it became in the hands of a culture shaped by decades of authoritarian control was something else.

If something bad happens to you, it is because of misdeeds in a previous life. Accept it. Reflect on it. Do not resist it — resistance only generates more bad karma. Respect your elders, your teachers, your monks, regardless of what they do, because the position deserves deference even when the person does not.

Do not get involved in politics. Live quietly. Accumulate merit. Please those in authority over you.

It played out in precise detail, in a country I know personally, within living memory.

The Buddha's teaching that suffering is universal and demands compassion became: your suffering is your own karmic debt. The teaching of non-attachment became: do not attach yourself to justice or freedom. The teaching of respect became: unconditional deference to authority, regardless of what that authority does.

The tradition did not create this. The tradition was used.

* * *

Indifference Is Not Neutral

If there is a common thread running through the worst and most durable systems of oppression in human history, it is not only the cruelty of the people who built them. It is the indifference of the people who let them continue.

Any of us who looks away from injustice is not neutral. We are making a choice. The choice may be entirely rational given what they know will happen if they do not look away. The choice may be the product of three generations of training in exactly the survival strategy their family needed to stay alive.

It may be the only choice that feels available.

The dictator does not need everyone to support him. He only needs enough people to be afraid enough not to oppose him. Fear produces indifference. Indifference produces longevity. Longevity produces the next generation trained in the same fear, the same indifference, the same silence. And the cycle continues — not because anyone chose it but because no one chose to interrupt it.

But the indifference this chapter is describing is not only the product of fear. That is important to name. The person standing at the roadside in Myanmar has a reason for their compliance that is specific and brutal — they have seen what happens to those who do not comply.

Their indifference was installed through the direct experience of violence and its consequences. That kind of indifference deserves compassion alongside its honest examination.

There is another kind of indifference that is harder to excuse — though I include myself in this. The indifference of comfort. Most of us know, at some level, that somewhere not far from where we live, something is wrong. A community that is struggling. A person who is suffering. A situation that our attention and our voice might help. And most of us, without the compulsion of fear, without the threat of disappearing in the night, decide — not dramatically, not cruelly, just quietly — that today is not the day to let it fully in.

This indifference is not a prison built by someone else. It is a prison built by the self. The walls are not soldiers and surveillance. They are the comfort that makes looking away feel like a reasonable choice rather than a moral one. The news cycle that provides the feeling of awareness without the demand of response.

Both prisons produce the same outcome. The suffering continues. The person who looks away out of fear and the person who looks away out of comfort are not morally equivalent. One is a prisoner. The other chose the cell. But both are absent from the contest. And the contest is decided by who shows up.

* * *

Leaving

I was lucky. That needs to be said before anything else. Born into a family that had rebuilt itself after losing everything, that had managed to create enough stability to give a child access to education, to medicine, to the possibility of a different future. Lucky in the way that feels unearned — which is the only way luck ever feels when you are standing next to people who have none.

I became a doctor. I tutored students. I worked inside a system that the regime had systematically dismantled — underfunded, underpaid, structured to reward compliance and punish excellence. I earned less than a driver. Not because the work mattered less but because the system was not designed to reward work. It was designed to reward proximity to power.

I wanted a better life. I wanted to be able to support my parents when they grew old. I came to Australia. Six years in Alice Springs first — the kind of posting that teaches you things about yourself that comfortable postings never could. Then a city. A career. The gradual construction of a life that looked, from the outside, like the one I had come to build.

And underneath it, always, the guilt.

Not the dramatic guilt of someone who had abandoned a cause. The quieter, more persistent guilt of someone who had chosen their own survival — their own parents, their own future — while friends and colleagues were still inside.

While the coup came. While the country collapsed again, the brief democratic opening slammed shut, the military back in control, the people who had dared to hope paying the price for having hoped.

* * *

The Colleague's Words

One day a colleague reached out. Someone still inside, still fighting, part of the resistance that had refused to accept the coup as the end of the story.

He said thank you.

The Starlink equipment I had funded — the satellite internet terminals that let the resistance communicate across a country where the regime had shut down the networks. The hospital supplies. The funds I dedicate every month to the revolution and to humanitarian assistance, because it is the only thing I know how to do from here that makes any difference from there.

He said they would not still be there without it.

I told him about the guilt. About choosing my parents over the fight. About the cowardice I had been carrying. About the feeling that everything I had done from the outside was inadequate compared to what the people on the inside were risking.

He was quiet for a moment. Then he said: your donation is significant. It is driving our cause. It is saving lives. You are doing more from there than you could do from here. We have plenty of people who are here.

We do not have enough people who are there and still connected to us. Do not beat yourself up. Perhaps we are all pieces of a puzzle. What we need — all of us, here and there — is to conquer our fear.

I have thought about those words many times since.

* * *

All a Puzzle

Perhaps we are all pieces of a puzzle.

That sentence does something to the guilt. Not because it removes the weight of what is happening —

nothing removes that weight — but because it reframes what contribution means. The person on the front line and the person sending resources from abroad are not in a hierarchy of moral worth.

They are in a system. A system that requires different things from different people in different positions.

Breaking the cycle of fear and indifference does not require everyone to become Aung San Suu Kyi. It requires enough people to find the specific form of resistance available from their specific position — and to take it.

The one who leaves and finds ways to contribute from a distance. The journalist who stays and documents. The student who protests. The parent who raises their child with the question rather than the compliance.

All pieces. All necessary. None sufficient alone.

But how does a piece of the puzzle actually move? How does a person whose dial has been stuck — by fear, by training, by three generations of learned indifference — find their way back to the conscience that was always there underneath it?

The answer, it turns out, is not willpower. It is not a moral decision made in the abstract. It is almost always a moment of contact. A specific person. A specific reality. Made concrete and close enough that the abstraction breaks and the other person's experience registers as real — as real as your own.

That is the mechanism. It has always been the mechanism. Not instruction. Not ideology. Contact. The willingness to let what is happening to someone else be as urgent and as specific as what is happening to you.

The puzzle does not move by trying harder. It moves the moment you let another person's reality in.

* * *

Freedom from Fear

Aung San Suu Kyi said the only real prison is fear. What she meant, I think, is not that fear is irrational. Fear in Myanmar was entirely rational. The consequences of resistance were real. The fear was not a distortion of reality. It was a correct reading of it.

What she meant is that the person who acts from fear — who makes every choice based on what the system will do to them if they step out of line — has handed the system something more valuable than their compliance. They have handed it their capacity to act from conscience rather than calculation. Their ability to be, in any meaningful sense, free.

Freedom from fear does not mean the absence of fear. It means acting from something larger than fear even when the fear is present. Choosing, in the specific situation you are in, the action that the moral instinct requires — not because it is safe, but because the alternative is to become the kind of person who only does what is safe.

I did not choose the country I was born in. I did not choose the history I inherited. I did not choose the fear that was installed in me before I had words for it. But I had, and I have, the choice of what to do with it.

All we need is to conquer our fear.

Not all at once. Not heroically. But in the specific, available, particular way that each person — from their specific position, with their specific resources, shaped by their specific history — can choose to stop looking away.

Stop looking away.

The puzzle needs every piece.

CHAPTER SIX

The Dream and the Machine

Every movement that has ever tried to change the world began with a genuine moral observation. Something is wrong. Something could be better. The people in charge have failed to see it or have chosen not to.

That observation did not stay an observation. It drove people to act. To organise. To overthrow what existed and replace it with something they believed would be better. Across every century and every continent, human beings have attempted to build the world the conscience pointed toward — the world of harmony, equity, and shared dignity that has never quite arrived but has never stopped being attempted.

Those attempts are the political history of the world. That history, looked at honestly, tells a story with three recurring elements. The genuine idea that began each system. The hunger for power that captured it. And the good will that failed anyway — not through corruption, but through the gap between what was designed and what human beings, in all their complexity, actually did with it.

Understanding all three is what it takes to think clearly about politics. Miss the first and you become cynical. Miss the second and you become naive. Miss the third and you become self-righteous.

* * *

In the Beginning

Before ideology, before written law, before any of the systems that political philosophy has argued over for centuries, there was a simpler arrangement. The tribe. The village. The community small enough that everyone knew everyone, that leadership was visible and its consequences immediate.

The first leaders were not elected and did not inherit their position. They earned it. The best hunter. The most experienced warrior. The elder whose judgment had proven reliable across enough seasons to be trusted with the next one.

Their authority was practical and revocable. A chief who led his people into starvation or defeat did not need to be voted out. He was replaced by whoever proved more capable.

Then the communities grew. And the feedback loop broke.

When a leader governs a village of two hundred people, everyone can see what he does and what it produces. When a king governs a kingdom of two million, most of them will never see him at all. The distance between the decision and its consequence grew until accountability became practically impossible. And into that distance — as into every vacuum of accountability — power flowed and filled it.

The solution every large society independently arrived at was the same. Divine right. The king was not answerable to the people because his authority did not come from the people. It came from God. The same mechanism that captured religion captured governance simultaneously. Sacred language placed around power to make it unchallengeable.

The prophet was the original disruptor of this arrangement. Moses confronting Pharaoh. Jesus overturning the tables of the money changers. Muhammad challenging the tribal hierarchies of Arabia. The Buddha refusing the caste system.

In each case the founder's original act was a challenge to the alliance of religious and political power. And in each case the institution that formed around the founder eventually rebuilt the alliance the founder had dismantled.

* * *

The Genuine Idea

By the time the modern era arrived the divine right of kings had been sufficiently discredited that new justifications for governance were needed. And into that space came the great political ideologies. Each one a genuine attempt to answer the question: how do we organise human beings justly?

Communism began with a moral observation that was entirely correct. The industrial revolution had produced extraordinary wealth. That wealth was being generated by the labour of millions of people who received almost none of it.

Workers lived in conditions of poverty and degradation that were not the product of their own failure but of a system designed to extract maximum value from their labour while returning minimum value to their lives.

Marx looked at this and said the problem was the structure of ownership itself. Collective ownership. No one profits from the labour of another. The class hierarchy abolished by design.

The idea was genuine. The execution produced some of the worst tyrannies in human history. The Soviet Union. Maoist China. Cambodia under the Khmer Rouge. North Korea. Each began with genuine revolutionaries.

Each produced, within years or decades, a new hierarchy as rigid and as brutal as the one it replaced — with the added feature that it could not be challenged even in theory, because the revolution had declared itself the final answer and dissent had become treason.

Socialism has meant different things in different places. But the historical record is consistent enough to demand honest examination.

Large-scale attempts at fully centralised socialist systems — state ownership of production, centralised planning, the removal of market mechanisms — have often struggled seriously wherever tried. Not only because corruption followed reliably, but because no central authority has ever proven capable of processing the extraordinary complexity of information that a functioning economy requires.

Venezuela attempted a version of it with its oil wealth as the foundation.

The result — shaped by a combination of policy choices, oil dependency, corruption, external pressures, and governance failures — included economic collapse, mass emigration, and a population reduced to scarcity within a generation.

What is often described as socialist success — the Nordic model — is, on closer examination, something quite different. These are capitalist economies with robust private markets, strong property rights, and competitive corporations operating globally.

What distinguishes them is not the absence of the market but the strength of the democratic institutions built around it.

High taxation redistributes wealth generated by capitalism. Strong unions give workers genuine negotiating power. The lesson of the Nordic model is not that socialism works. It is that capitalism, when embedded in strong democratic institutions with genuine accountability and a culture of civic trust, can be made to serve human dignity rather than simply accumulate wealth.

Democracy made the most honest assessment of human nature of any system ever designed. It did not assume that leaders would be good. It assumed they would not be — and built in the corrections accordingly.

Elections.

Separation of powers. Free press. Independent courts. The entire architecture of democratic governance is, at its root, a system designed to work even when the people running it are not good. That is its genius. And its precise vulnerability.

* * *

The Hunger for Power

While the idealist was drawing the blueprint, someone else was always in the room.

Not reading the blueprint for what it promised the people. Reading it for what it offered the person who controlled it. The reach. The authority. The extraordinary leverage that comes from standing at the center of a system that organises the lives of millions.

This person appears in every organisation, at every level, whenever authority exists long enough to discover it can be redirected.

He is the revolutionary who fought genuinely for liberation and then, once the old power was gone, looked at the empty seat and sat down in it. The democrat who ran on the will of the people and spent his tenure dismantling the structures that might one day hold him accountable.

He is not always a monster at the beginning. Sometimes he begins as a genuine believer. The corruption is rarely a single dramatic moment of choosing evil. It is a series of small adjustments, each individually justifiable, that accumulate over time into a person who has become what they once opposed.

Robespierre genuinely believed in the French Revolution. He also sent thousands to the guillotine in the name of its purity. Stalin genuinely believed in the liberation of the working class. He also murdered millions of them when they became inconvenient to his power. The belief and the corruption coexisted.

But the hunger for power is only one part of the story. And focusing on it too narrowly leads to a comfortable mistake — the assumption that the problem is always the bad actor who entered the system with bad intentions. Remove the bad actor, the thinking goes, and the system works as designed.

It does not. Because the system does not only attract the corrupt. It produces them.

Think of the person who entered the system with genuine purpose. The young policy officer who joined the public service because they believed good government could change lives. The social worker who went into the work because they had seen what neglect did to children and could not stand by. The politician who started with a real conviction about what their community needed.

It does not confront these people dramatically. It works on them slowly, through accumulation. The first compromise is small and individually reasonable — a report softened here because the timing is politically inconvenient, a finding delayed there because the minister needs managing.

And then one day — not through any single dramatic moment of choosing wrong, but through the weight of a thousand small adjustments — the person who entered the institution to serve the people it was built for is now defending it against those people. Protecting the process. Speaking the language of the system rather than the language of the person it was supposed to serve.

They are not lying. They are not cynical. They have simply, gradually, become what the system needed them to become. It does not need monsters. It just needs enough time, enough pressure, and enough small compromises to do its work.

The most dangerous leader is not the one who is openly corrupt. The openly corrupt can be recognised and opposed. The most dangerous is the one who has genuinely merged his own continuation in power with the continuation of the cause he claims to serve.

* * *

The Flaw at the Foundation

And so we arrive at democracy. The form of government specifically designed to prevent everything described in this chapter so far. It looked at the problem — power corrupting, institutions serving themselves, rulers becoming what they were meant to constrain — and tried to build the correction into the architecture itself.

Because the fact that even the most carefully designed system for constraining power is vulnerable to the same hollowing out that destroyed every less careful system before it is not a minor observation.

Not that democracy is no better than dictatorship — it is enormously better, and the difference matters in the daily lives of the people living inside it. But no arrangement, however well designed, is immune to what this book has been tracing. Because none of them run themselves. They all run on human beings. And human beings bring their full capacity for both good and harm into everything they build.

Democracy counts the vote. That is its genius and its flaw simultaneously. It says the legitimacy of governance comes from the consent of the governed. That principle is the most important political idea human beings have ever developed. It can also become indifferent to the quality of the choice being made.

The vote of the person who has studied the candidates and chosen with the long-term good of the community in mind counts exactly the same as the vote of the person who chose based on fear of the other group. The informed vote and the manipulated vote are identical in the counting. Democracy does not reward wisdom. It rewards numbers.

And numbers can be manufactured. Not by fraud alone but by the far more effective method of manufacturing the emotions that drive people to vote. Fear. Anger. The sense that the other group is coming for what is yours. The politician who understands this has found the most powerful engine in democratic politics. Not the best policy. The best enemy.

Division creates hate. And hate is more powerful than love as a political mobilising force. Love is quiet. It does not march. It does not send money at midnight in response to an outrage. Hate arrives fast and burns hot and brings people out in numbers that no positive vision has ever quite matched.

It is worth acknowledging what democracy has achieved, because the critique above should not obscure it. Democratic societies have been responsible for remarkable expansions of human freedom and dignity — the abolition of slavery, universal suffrage, the welfare state, legal protections for minorities.

These happened because enough people inside democratic systems demanded that the system live up to its own stated values.

The critique is not that democracy has failed. It is that it requires constant maintenance from the people inside it. And that maintenance is precisely what fear and indifference erode.

* * *

The Silence of the Good

The silence of the good people deserves its own examination.

I have been one of these people. There have been moments — in Myanmar, in Australia, in the daily accumulation of small decisions about where to look and where to turn away — when I chose the comfort of not knowing over the discomfort of knowing and being required to act. I am writing this book partly because I got tired of being that person.

Hate is loud. It fills the comment sections and the rallies and the airwaves. It is confident and certain and always looking for an audience. The person who believes in something quieter tends not to march.

Tends not to donate at midnight. Tends to trust that the system will correct itself. That decency will prevail without their particular intervention. That the institutions will hold.

They are often wrong about this.

Most of us, remaining silent and assuming the best, have watched in country after country as the loud and the hateful and the strategically divisive accumulated enough votes to put into power someone who then proceeded to dismantle the very institutions we trusted to protect us.

If there is a common thread in democracies that have failed or come close to failing, it is not only the cruelty of the people who attacked the institutions. It is the indifference of those of us who trusted those institutions to defend themselves.

In several countries over recent decades researchers and international observers have documented a similar sequence. A democracy that appeared stable losing its accountability structures not through coup or revolution but through the gradual accumulation of legal changes — each individually defensible, cumulatively transformative. Courts changed. Media environments shifted. Electoral rules were redrawn. In each case the people who valued what was being lost tended to assume that the institutions would protect themselves. In each case the institutions required active defence from the people inside them. The gap between those two assumptions — that the system will hold versus that the system needs holding — has been the decisive margin.

> *The good people stayed home because they trusted the system. The hateful people showed up because they wanted to change it. The system cannot tell the difference. It only counts who came.*

Mandatory voting changes some of this calculation. When everyone must vote the silent majority can no longer remain silent. But mandatory voting is not sufficient on its own. A vote cast without understanding is a vote for whoever managed to reach that person last, with the most emotional message, in the least amount of time.

* * *

What Functional Democracy Actually Requires

Functional democracy requires something no electoral system can manufacture. Citizens who understand the system they are participating in. Who know enough about how power works to make choices that serve their actual interests rather than their momentary emotions. Who can distinguish between the leader genuinely trying to solve the problem and the leader using the problem to consolidate power.

That is not a standard most democracies have come close to meeting. Not because citizens are stupid. Because the systems that would produce that kind of informed citizenship — the education, the free press, the civic culture — are exactly the systems that the person who benefits from uninformed voting has every incentive to undermine.

Freedom comes at a price. The price is not paid at the ballot box. It is paid in the ongoing, unglamorous, often invisible work of building and maintaining the culture that makes the ballot box mean something.

The educated citizen. The independent press. The trusted structure. The norm that says the loser accepts the result and the winner does not use victory to make future losing impossible.

These things are not guaranteed by the system. They are produced by the people inside it.

And sometimes they have been produced. That is not a small thing. The peaceful transfer of power after a lost election — requiring the losing side to accept a result they dispute, to trust a process they could reject — has happened thousands of times across dozens of countries. Rights have been extended to people excluded when the system was designed. Courts have ruled against the governments that appointed them. Institutions have held under pressure from the very people who led them.

This is the evidence that the system can work as designed — that people inside it have, in enough moments, chosen the institution over themselves, the long term over the immediate advantage. That is the record alongside the one this chapter has been examining.

* * *

The Pattern, Again

Look at what we have now. The tribe grown into the kingdom that served the king and called it God's will. The revolutionary movement become the new hierarchy. The democracy designed for human imperfection being hollowed out by exactly the imperfection it was designed to contain.

The sequence across all of these systems is the same. A genuine moral impulse. Power getting inside it. The meaning draining away while the structure remains.

The system does not save us. We save the system. By refusing, one choice at a time, to let it become something the people who built it would not recognise.

That choice is always available. In this moment. To the person reading this.

CHAPTER SEVEN

What Kind of Creature Are We?

What kind of creature are we actually dealing with?

Not the idealised version that religion has sometimes imagined — a soul temporarily housed in flesh, oriented toward the divine, capable of transcendence if properly instructed. Not the cynical version that a casual reading of history might suggest — a violent, tribal, self-interested animal dressing its appetites in the language of principle. Something more complicated and more interesting than either.

A creature that has passed through extraordinary transformations across three hundred thousand years and arrived here carrying all of them simultaneously. Layered on top of each other inside the same body, the same nervous system, the same dial.

The hunter. The farmer. The believer. The philosopher. The citizen. The algorithm-fed consumer of the twenty-first century. All of them present. All of them occasionally in conflict. None of them fully replaced by the next.

Understanding that layering is the beginning of understanding why the same failures keep recurring across centuries and cultures. Not because most of us are stupid. Because these are expressions of biology operating inside conditions it was not designed for.

* * *

The Phases We Have Passed Through

We did not arrive here in a single leap. We moved through stages — each one building on the last, each one leaving its residue in the creatures we became. The hunter-gatherer is still inside the office worker. The tribal instinct is still inside the global citizen. Understanding the layers does not excuse what they produce. But it makes it comprehensible.

For roughly two hundred and fifty thousand of our three hundred thousand years, human beings lived in small nomadic bands of twenty to fifty people. No fixed home. No kings, no priests, no taxes. Leadership was informal and earned daily.

This is who we are at the deepest level. A social animal calibrated for a world of fifty people, immediate consequences, and relationships maintained by daily contact. That moral instinct worked naturally here — not because people were more virtuous but because the feedback loop between action and consequence was short enough that cruelty had immediate social cost.

About twelve thousand years ago something changed that altered everything that followed. Human beings stopped following food and started growing it. Fixed settlements appeared. Population exploded. Surplus food meant some people could stop farming and start specialising.

For the first time in human experience, the person making decisions affecting thousands of people did not live inside the consequences of those decisions.

The distance between power and accountability was born here. And into that distance, as this book has argued from the beginning, everything that corrupts followed.

The city and the empire extended that distance further still. Each required a story — a moral or ideological framework — to motivate its own people and justify its expansion to itself. Every empire needed a story.

And every empire fell. Overextension. Internal corruption. Loss of the founding story. The consistency is hard to ignore.

The industrial revolution compressed everything. In two centuries it produced more material change than the previous ten thousand years. The moral and philosophical traditions that had evolved slowly across millennia were suddenly operating inside a world of mass production, global trade, industrialised warfare, and cities of millions.

They were not built for it. Neither were we. And now the information age has given every element of human nature — the generous and the cruel, the wise and the manipulable — a global platform and an algorithm designed to amplify whichever generates the most engagement.

* * *

The Ideas We Developed to Make Sense of It

Alongside the physical and organisational evolution, human beings were trying to think their way through the conditions they found themselves in. The philosophical traditions that emerged across different cultures and different centuries are the accumulated attempts of the most serious human thinkers across three thousand years to answer questions that have not changed. How should a human being live? What do we owe each other? Where does meaning come from?

What is remarkable is how often, across traditions that had no contact with each other, the answers converge. Different maps. The same territory.

The oldest tradition — mythological and animist thought — placed human beings inside a web of relationships and obligations that extended beyond the human. It required humility. The recognition that the world was not made for us. The first expression of the conscience reaching beyond the immediate self.

Around 2,500 years ago something extraordinary happened across Asia simultaneously. Buddhism taught that the root of all suffering is the illusion of a fixed self that must be protected at all costs.

Compassion for all beings is not an advanced practice in Buddhism.

It is the beginning. Taoism said wisdom is learning to move with the natural flow of things rather than against them. Confucianism said society holds together through genuine moral obligation to strangers, to the community, to the broader social fabric. The thread connecting all of them — the self is not the center, the suffering of others is real, wisdom is the capacity to act from something larger than immediate self-interest.

In Greece at roughly the same time, the radical idea that reason — not gods, not tradition — could be used to examine how the world works and how life should be lived. Socrates spent his life asking questions rather than providing answers.

The Athenians executed him for it.

The Stoics produced perhaps the most practically useful philosophy ever developed. Divide everything in your life into what is within your control and what is not. Your thoughts, your responses, your character

— within.

Everything else — outside. Wisdom is making this distinction clearly and focusing entirely on the first.

Nihilism is the void that appears when the old frameworks collapse. Nothing is inherently meaningful. Nothing is objectively right or wrong. Nietzsche was not a nihilist — he was terrified of nihilism and spent his entire career trying to find a way past it.

He saw it as the inevitable consequence of the death of the God-framework. And a civilisation that has lost its moral foundation without replacing it is not liberated. It is lost.

Existentialism is the response. Yes, the universe is silent on the question of meaning. That is not despair — it is freedom. You exist first and then define yourself through your choices and commitments.

Camus put it most directly — life is absurd, meaning is not given, and yet we must imagine Sisyphus happy. The pushing is the point. The refusal to stop is the act of meaning-making itself.

Humanism holds that human dignity is real and requires no theological justification to be true. That sense was there before the doctrine. The doctrine is valuable to the extent that it honours the conscience. When it overrides the conscience in service of institutional authority, it has lost the thing that made it worth following.

* * *

The Structures We Built

The band worked because everyone knew everyone and accountability was immediate. The tribe required more formal leadership but retained enough personal connection that bad leadership was still visible.

The chiefdom introduced hereditary power for the first time — someone had to manage the agricultural surplus, and the person who managed it gained power that passed to offspring rather than the most capable next person.

The feedback loop between leadership and accountability began to lengthen here. It has been lengthening ever since.

The city-state produced the most intense flowering of political and philosophical experimentation in human history precisely because it was small enough for accountability to remain real. The empire solved the problem of scale but required permanent military force to maintain itself and had no reliable mechanism for peaceful transfer of power. Every empire in history eventually collapsed — usually from the inside.

Democracy made the most honest assessment of human nature of any system ever designed. It did not assume that leaders would be good. It assumed they would not be — and built in the corrections accordingly.

It has proven the most durable solution. And it has also proven vulnerable to the same erosion — the form maintained while the substance drains away.

Supranational organisations — the United Nations, the European Union, the International Criminal Court — are the newest and most fragile experiment. The recognition that some problems cannot be solved by individual nation-states acting alone.

Still deeply contested. The tension between national sovereignty and the global accountability that the most serious human problems now require is one of the defining conflicts of our moment.

* * *

Has Moral Standing Ever Been Enough?

This is the question that sits at the heart of human history and deserves an honest answer. Not the comforting answer. The true one.

Has there ever been a truly peaceful, morally advanced group that survived sustained hostile pressure through the power of its values alone? A community that held to genuine compassion, genuine non-violence, genuine philosophical commitment to the dignity of every person — and survived intact against a force willing to use organised violence without moral restraint?

Not one. Not anywhere. Not permanently.

The early Buddhists survived because a warrior king — Ashoka — chose to protect them. Without his armies, Buddhism would likely have been absorbed or destroyed. The Jains have survived 2,500 years but by occupying an economic niche that made them useful to rulers.

The Cathars of twelfth century southern France were exterminated within a generation. The Quakers in Pennsylvania lasted about seventy years before the political reality of the surrounding world made pure pacifism untenable.

Every peaceful, morally advanced community that survived did so through protection by a powerful patron, irrelevance to power, or selective pacifism within a larger system of violence they depended on for their safety.

Let that sit for a moment. Pure moral goodness has not historically been a shield against organised violence. Not once. Not in any recorded case.

> *Moral purity does not protect you from violence. It never has. The person of genuine conscience and the person willing to kill them are not in a fair contest. History records the outcome consistently.*

And yet. Something else is also true.

The people die. The ideas do not always die with them.

Buddhism survived because it spread widely enough that no single act of destruction could reach all of it simultaneously. Socrates was executed. His ideas survived through Plato and changed the course of Western thought for two and a half thousand years.

But not all ideas survive.

Not all knowledge systems survive the destruction of their carriers. The Cathars are gone permanently. The stolen generations policy in Australia was specifically designed to sever the transmission between Aboriginal parents and their children — to prevent the knowledge, the language, the ceremony from passing to the next generation. It worked in significant measure. Some knowledge is gone permanently.

The ideas that survive annihilation tend to be widely distributed, abstract enough to be carried by new people in new contexts, and universal enough that they can be rediscovered even by people who have no connection to the original community.

The most universal expressions of the moral instinct — that every person carries dignity, that cruelty is wrong, that the suffering of others matters — have proven extraordinarily difficult to permanently extinguish. They keep being rediscovered because they are true in a way available to any person willing to look honestly at their own experience.

But the people who held them were lost first. Before the ideas. Before the question of what survived could even be asked.

Moral standing is not a strategy for survival against organised violence. It is orientation. The knowledge of what is right even when doing right carries cost. And it is the only force in human history that has ever actually expanded the circle — slowly, incompletely, at enormous cost to the people who carried it forward.

I find this conclusion uncomfortable. I would prefer to believe that moral clarity alone is sufficient. That the right values, held with enough conviction, protect the people who hold them. The history I know from the inside does not support that preference. So I try to hold the discomfort honestly rather than looking for a more comforting answer.

The people die. Some of the ideas survive. And occasionally — not always, not automatically — the ideas change what comes next.

* * *

What This Means for Everything That Follows

We are a creature carrying three hundred thousand years of accumulated experience inside the same nervous system that evolved to manage a band of fifty people around a fire.

We have developed extraordinary philosophical traditions and built organisational structures of breathtaking complexity. We have expanded the circle of who counts further than any previous generation imagined possible.

And the old instincts — the tribal default, the hunger for power, the capacity to dress self-interest in the language of the sacred — do not disappear. They are still here, in most of us, pressing against the moral framework that was built to contain them.

The stoic would say this is the condition. Not the tragedy. The condition. Accept what cannot be changed and focus entirely on what can. Which is the quality of your own response. The willingness to ask, in each situation, what the conscience actually requires rather than what the system is telling you to accept.

The existentialist would say the silence of the universe on the question of meaning is not an answer. It is an invitation. You are not pre-programmed. You choose. And the choice, made again and again in the small moments that accumulate into a life, is the only thing that has ever actually changed anything.

The humanist would say human dignity is real. It does not require divine authority to be true. It requires only the willingness to look honestly at another person and recognise what you see.

And what was present before any of these traditions named it — that keeps reappearing after every institution built to honour it has failed — would say something simpler than any of them.

You already know. You have always known.

The question is only whether you are willing to act on what you know.

The conscience came first. Everything else is what we did with it.

* * *

But knowing that better is worth fighting for and understanding how human beings have actually fought for it are two different things.

History is full of people who believed in better. Who saw the gap between what was and what they knew should be and decided the gap was no longer acceptable. Who organised, who resisted, who stood in front of power with nothing but conviction and the refusal to pretend that what was happening was right.

Some of them changed things. Some of them were destroyed. Most of them were forgotten entirely — their names unrecorded, their contributions invisible, their courage absorbed into the anonymous mass of human effort that slowly, impermanently, at enormous cost, moved the line.

What determined the difference between the revolution that produced something genuinely better and the one that simply replaced one domination with another?

CHAPTER EIGHT

The Rose and the Bullet

Myanmar sits in the heart of Southeast Asia, bordered by China to the north, Thailand to the east, India and Bangladesh to the west, and the Bay of Bengal to the south. It is a country of extraordinary natural beauty and extraordinary suffering. Home to over fifty million people and more than a hundred distinct ethnic groups, Myanmar has spent most of its modern history under military rule. That rule has used ethnic division, religious manipulation, and the systematic destruction of civil institutions to maintain its grip on a population that has never stopped trying to be free.

I was born there. I grew up there. I left. And I have spent the years since watching from the other side of the world as the country I came from was bombed, starved, imprisoned, and silenced — while the international community issued statements of deep concern and did not come.

Everything in this chapter is personal. Not in the sense that it is only my story — millions of people carry versions of it. But in the sense that the conscience buried under installed obedience, the moral tradition distorted into a tool of submission, the institution that serves power rather than the people it was built to protect — I did not learn these things from books alone.

I learned them standing at the side of a road at five in the morning.

* * *

I remember standing at the side of a road at five in the morning.

I was a state school student. We had been brought there in the dark, lined up along the street with the other children from the other schools, hands pressed together in the traditional greeting of reverence.

We were waiting for a general to pass.

Sometimes he passed in the morning. Sometimes we waited until noon and he passed then. We stood either way. We did not question it. It did not occur to us to question it.

Obedience had been installed in us so thoroughly and so early that it did not feel like obedience. It felt like the correct way to be.

That is what I want to tell you about how a military dictatorship actually works. Not the dramatic version — the arrests, the massacres, the disappeared. Those things happened. They are real and they are important.

But they are not the daily texture of life under a system designed to produce compliance.

The daily texture is a child standing in the dark waiting to wave at a general. Knowing without being told that this is what is required. Feeling, without being able to name it, that the world is organised around a hierarchy that cannot be questioned.

That feeling was not accidental. It was the product of a system that understood something about human beings that this book has been examining from the beginning. The most durable form of control is not the gun. It is the mind that no longer reaches for the door because it has forgotten there is a door.

* * *

What Made Myanmar Vulnerable

To understand how a military dictatorship takes root and holds for decades, you have to understand the specific soil it grew in. Because dictatorships are not simply imposed from outside. They grow from conditions that already exist.

The kingdom era had produced a society organised around hierarchy, obedience, and Buddhist practice as the primary framework for moral and social life. These were not weaknesses in themselves. The Buddhist monastic system provided education, social welfare, and moral authority. The cultural identity of the Bamar majority was coherent, proud, and ancient.

But the institutions of governance that produce democratic accountability — constitutional law, independent judiciary, a free press, a culture of political opposition as legitimate rather than treasonous — these had never had the conditions to develop. Not because the people lacked the capacity for them. But because the colonial period had no interest in building them.

This is not a criticism of Myanmar's cultures. It is a description of the specific vulnerability that colonialism encountered and exploited and then left behind in a condition that independence could not immediately repair.

* * *

The Flood of Ideas

Then the British arrived. And with them — not intentionally, not as a gift, but as an inevitable consequence of the contact — came the flood.

Socialism. Communism. Nationalism. Democracy. Self-determination. The rights of the individual against the state. For a generation of young Burmese students encountering for the first time the idea that the world as it was organised was not the world as it had to be — this flood of ideas was intoxicating.

The problem was not the ideas. The ideas were genuine and many of them were right. The problem was that the ideas arrived simultaneously — each movement with its own vision, its own followers, its own conviction that it alone understood what the country needed. That is not a failure of any one group. It is what happens when a people who have been denied political life for a generation are given it back all at once, without the time that negotiating a shared framework requires.

Elections are held. A parliament meets. Multiple parties, multiple ethnic groups, multiple ideological traditions — all of them legitimate, all of them with genuine constituencies — begin the slow and difficult work of negotiating what kind of country this will be.

That negotiation takes time. More time than a fragile new government, still building its foundations, had been given. The plurality was not a problem to be solved. It was the reality of what Myanmar actually was — a country of many peoples and many visions. But a military institution watching this complexity saw not a country in the process of becoming itself. It saw an opportunity. The instability was the justification. And in too many cases, that instability had been encouraged by the very forces that then offered to end it.

* * *

The Ethnic Wound That Colonialism Engineered

And underneath all of it, the fault lines that the British had deliberately created.

Myanmar is not and has never been a single ethnic entity. The Bamar majority share the country with the Karen, the Shan, the Kachin, the Chin, the Mon, the Rakhine, and dozens of smaller groups — each with their own language, their own cultural identity, their own relationship to the central state.

The British managed these groups through deliberate division. Recruiting Karen and Kachin soldiers into the colonial army while treating the Bamar majority with greater suspicion. Building a resentment economy — a system in which different groups competed for colonial favour and learned to see each other as competitors rather than compatriots.

Independence did not dissolve these divisions. It inherited them. The Panglong Agreement that Aung San negotiated in 1947 was a genuine attempt to build something different — a federal union in which ethnic minorities would have genuine autonomy.

It was the most important document in Myanmar's political history. And it was effectively buried with the man who created it, assassinated six months before independence at the age of thirty-two.

* * *

How Power Found Its Opening

Into this specific combination — multiple groups, multiple ideologies, multiple ethnic constituencies all negotiating simultaneously, a new government that had not yet had the time to build the institutions that protect democratic systems, and a military that had been the one functioning national structure throughout the independence struggle — into this, the hunger for power found its opening. Not because the people had failed. Because power does not wait for negotiations to finish.

Ne Win had fought for independence. He had genuine nationalist credentials. But what he did with the power he seized was monstrous. The atrocities of his rule — the decades of isolation, the suppression of every voice that dissented, the destruction of institutions that might have produced something better, the ethnic campaigns that killed and displaced hundreds of thousands — none of this can be softened or explained away. He was a monster. The conditions that allowed him to take power do not change what he chose to do with it.

And then something worse happened. The succession proved that military rule in Myanmar does not produce correction. It produces escalation. Than Shwe, who followed, was crueller than Ne Win. Min Aung Hlaing, who came after, was crueller still.

But the story between Ne Win and Min Aung Hlaing is not simply a straight line of oppression. It contains a moment of genuine hope — and the military's response to it reveals everything about what the institution is.

In 1988, after decades of Ne Win's rule had ground the country into poverty and fear, the people rose. Students. Workers. Monks. Hundreds of thousands in the streets. The military killed at least three thousand of them. But the protests forced Ne Win to step down. And facing international pressure, the new junta made a promise: free elections.

In 1990, the NLD won 392 of 492 seats. A landslide so decisive it should have been beyond dispute. The military ignored it completely. They arrested Aung San Suu Kyi. They declared the result void. And they continued to rule as if the election had never happened.

For the next two decades, the country remained under military dictatorship while Suu Kyi spent years in prison and under house arrest. Then in 2008, facing international pressure and wanting foreign investment, they produced a new constitution — designed not to enable democracy but to permanently protect military power within it. Twenty-five percent of parliamentary seats were reserved for unelected military officers by constitutional guarantee. Any amendment required more than seventy-five percent approval — which the military's reserved block alone could prevent. The commander-in-chief was given authority the president could not override. Suu Kyi was specifically barred from the presidency. The constitution was passed during Cyclone Nargis, while the country was in disaster, with a claimed approval rate of ninety-three percent.

In 2010 they held elections under this constitution. The NLD boycotted. The military's party won. A former general became president of what was presented to the world as a democratic transition.

What the generals had decided was that they could afford to let the NLD participate — because even if the NLD won, the constitution guaranteed the military could not lose. They miscalculated.

In 2015 the NLD won a landslide. In 2020 they won an even bigger one. The people had seen the opening and walked through it with complete conviction. The military's own party was obliterated. And Aung San Suu Kyi — the woman they had imprisoned, the daughter of the independence hero — was governing the country they had promised themselves they would never lose.

When the 2020 election produced a landslide for the civilian government — a result so decisive that even the military's own proxy party was obliterated — he demanded to be appointed president. The elected government refused. And so he took the country by force, arrested the elected leaders, and declared the result of the democratic vote fraudulent. A man rejected by his own country seized it at gunpoint.

What followed has been five years of darkness. Bombing of civilian villages. The killing of thousands of innocent people — children, elderly, women, men — without distinction, without limit, without mercy. Human rights abused in ways that defy description. Mutilation. Torture. Homes and entire communities razed and burned to the ground. A country dragged backwards by a man who could not accept that the people did not want him.

After five years of this, he staged an election designed to have only one possible outcome. He passed a law banning the NLD — the party that had won the 2020 landslide — and dissolved it. Opposition leaders were in prison or dead. The election was held in December 2025 and January 2026, with voting impossible in large parts of the country already seized by resistance forces. His military-backed party won in a landslide. In April 2026, he was inaugurated as president — a parliament he had engineered voting him in with 429 out of 500 votes.

A man the people rejected in 2020 has given himself the title they refused him. On the bones of the country he destroyed to take it.

That is not governance. That is not even tyranny in the organised sense. That is a man burning down everything around him so that the ruins confirm his necessity.

That is not a military protecting its nation. That is a man protecting his ego. And millions of people are paying for it with their lives, their homes, and their futures.

That is what we are dealing with.

And what have we left to negotiate.

He was wrong. But he had the guns. And in the absence of institutions strong enough to constrain him, the guns were what mattered.

The strong hand takes. It does not give back.

* * *

The Woman Who Refused

Aung San Suu Kyi did not choose to become the symbol of a revolution. She came back to Myanmar in

1988 to care for her dying mother. What she understood, arriving back in a country erupting in protest, was something simpler and more demanding than political strategy.

She understood that the fear had to be broken. And that the only way to break the fear was to demonstrate, visibly and personally, that it was possible to stand in front of the machine without becoming either its servant or its mirror.

She chose non-violence not as a tactical calculation but as a moral commitment. You cannot build a just society with unjust means. The revolution that uses the methods of the tyranny it is fighting tends to produce a new tyranny wearing different clothes.

She gave everything to this commitment. Her marriage — her husband died of cancer in England while she remained under house arrest, refusing to leave because she knew the military would never allow her to return.

Her freedom — fifteen years of house arrest before 2010, then a brief return to the world she had fought for, then arrested again in 2021 when the military took back what the people had won. As of this writing she remains in detention, her sentence a number no eighty-year-old should ever have to hear. Her safety — on multiple occasions the military arranged situations that could easily have ended in her death, and she walked into them without flinching.

In 1989, under house arrest for the first time, she was offered release on the condition that she leave Myanmar permanently. She refused.

* * *

The Peaceful Resistance That Failed

The peaceful resistance of the people of Myanmar did not fail once. It failed repeatedly, across decades, at enormous human cost.

1988 — the student uprising. Massacred. Thousands dead. The military consolidated rather than retreated.

1990 — the election. Won by the NLD in a landslide. Annulled.

2007 — the Saffron Revolution. Buddhist monks leading mass protests. The military shot monks in the street. The protests were crushed.

2021 — after the coup, the largest sustained civil disobedience movement in Myanmar's history. Millions marching. Young people standing in front of soldiers with flowers and signs. The military shot them. And kept shooting.

At each of these moments the logic of non-violent resistance was tested. And at each moment the military demonstrated that it was prepared to absorb the moral cost, the international condemnation, and the domestic grief, in order to maintain its position.

> *Moral purity does not protect you from violence. It never has. The person of genuine conscience and the person willing to kill them are not in a fair contest. History records the outcome consistently.*

* * *

What She Actually Achieved

And yet when I think of her something happens that no political analysis can fully account for.

Not admiration exactly. Something more immediate than admiration. An urge. To do right. To protect someone who needs protecting. To give something rather than accumulate something. To be ethical not because the calculation favours it but because the alternative — becoming the kind of person who only acts when the calculation favours it — is a form of dying that leaves the body intact.

That urge is not a political response to a political figure. It is a moral response to a moral example. And it is, I think, the most important thing she actually achieved — more important than any election result, more durable than any political arrangement that will eventually be renegotiated or reversed.

She became a beacon. Not the kind that guides ships safely to harbour. The kind that simply burns. Visibly. Consistently. In conditions specifically designed to extinguish it. So that anyone who can see it knows that the thing it represents is real. That it exists. That it is possible to carry it.

The military understood this at some level. Why else spend so much effort confining her, isolating her, preventing her from being seen? A person without genuine moral authority does not require that kind of management. You only need to contain the light if the light is real.

What she did — across fifteen years of house arrest, across the decades of sacrifice, across the refusal to leave, the refusal to compromise, the refusal to accept the military's definition of what was possible — was demonstrate something that no argument, however well constructed, can demonstrate.

That the conscience is not theoretical. That a human being can actually live from it. Under conditions specifically designed to make living from it impossible. And keep living from it anyway.

When people see her — really see her, not as a political symbol but as a human being who chose dignity over safety and kept choosing it for decades — the thing that moves in them is not political opinion.

It is the recognition of something they already knew. That this is what the conscience looks like when it is not suppressed. That this is what a human being looks like when they live from the deepest thing they carry rather than the most convenient.

That recognition is not comfort. It is a demand. The conscience, once it sees itself reflected in another person who has honoured it at great cost, cannot comfortably return to the arrangements it made with fear and convenience. It has been shown what it is capable of. And that showing changes something.

The military imprisoned her body. It could not imprison what she demonstrated about human beings. That demonstration has moved the dial in ways that no election result could move it. It is one of the reasons the 2021 generation could name what was happening with a clarity the fear-constructed silence of earlier decades had made harder to speak aloud.

She did not fail. She planted something. In a country. In a generation. In every person who has ever seen her story and felt that urge — to do right, to protect, to give, to be ethical — and recognised in it something that was already in them, waiting.

The measure of what she achieved is not in the political outcomes that her sacrifice did not produce. It is in the moral evolution it did produce.

That is not nothing. Given everything this book has examined about how moral progress actually happens — slowly, impermanently, at enormous cost to the people who carry it forward — that is, in fact, everything.

* * *

The Rose Cannot Withstand a Bullet

At some point the conversation about peace becomes its own form of violence.

Myanmar has tried negotiation. For decades. Under every framework the international community could construct. Ceasefire agreements that the military signed and violated. Dialogue processes that the military entered in bad faith.

Every single one failed. Not because the people seeking peace were naive. Because one party to every negotiation was a military institution that had no intention of accepting any outcome that reduced its power.

You cannot negotiate peace with an institution that has decided peace means your permanent subjugation. You cannot split the difference between dignity and slavery and call the result a compromise.

* * *

The Poison in the Drink

There is a form of resistance that the world often holds up as the most morally elevated response to oppression. The hunger strike. The fast unto death. The willingness to offer your own body as the evidence of injustice.

It is genuinely brave. And in the right conditions it works. Bobby Sands in a British prison. Gandhi facing the Raj. In each case a person used their own suffering as a political instrument because the authority they were confronting had something to lose from their death — a reputation, a domestic legitimacy, an international standing.

Against a military dictatorship that has already decided your death is acceptable, the hunger strike is not a political instrument.

It is a gift.

The general does not need to wait for you to starve. He will put poison in the drink. He will arrange a medical emergency. He will let you die in a cell and report that you died of natural causes and dare the world to prove otherwise. And the world, which has already demonstrated its willingness to accept his version of events when accepting it is cheaper than investigating it, will move on.

Non-violence as a political strategy rests on a specific assumption. That the authority being confronted retains enough moral sensitivity — or enough political vulnerability — that the spectacle of peaceful people being harmed creates pressure that eventually exceeds the benefit of maintaining the arrangement being protested.

When that assumption is false — when the authority has specifically calculated that it can absorb the moral cost of killing peaceful people indefinitely — then non-violence as a strategy is not elevated.

It is ineffective.

And asking people to persist in an ineffective strategy indefinitely, in the name of moral purity, while they and their families are killed, is not a moral position. It is a comfortable one. Comfortable for the people asking. Not for the people dying.

* * *

The Comparisons That Do Not Hold

Gandhi's non-violence worked against the British Empire because the British had a democratic home politics sensitive to the moral cost of imperial violence. The Indian independence movement created genuine political pressure at home in Britain. The British had interests in the international order that made the cost of continued colonial rule eventually exceed the benefit.

Nelson Mandela spent twenty-seven years in prison while the ANC conducted both non-violent advocacy internationally and armed resistance inside South Africa simultaneously. The negotiated transition came when both sides concluded that continued conflict was more costly than resolution.

The civil rights movement operated inside a democracy whose founding documents explicitly contradicted the practices being protested. The images of peaceful marchers being attacked created shame that moved the political calculation of legislators.

In each case the non-violence worked because the specific conditions made it work.

The Myanmar military is not the British Raj. It is not the apartheid regime. It is not the segregated American South. It is an institution committed not merely to political control but to the permanent annihilation of the moral evolution that the people of Myanmar have undergone. An institution that has rewritten the constitution to guarantee its own power and has demonstrated that it will kill however many people are necessary to maintain it.

An institution with that specific goal is not a negotiating partner. It is an existential threat. And responding to an existential threat with a request for peaceful negotiation is not wisdom. It is the demand that the person with the gun pointed at their head hold still so the shooting is easier.

Do you want us to be slaves for the sake of peace?

Do you want us to be slaves for the sake of peace?

That question deserves to sit on the page without an answer provided by someone else. Because it is not a rhetorical question. It is the real question. The one that the international community's requests for restraint are implicitly answering yes to without saying so out loud.

That answer should be named for what it is. Not peace. The demand for surrender wearing peace's clothes.

* * *

What the Society Became Through Suffering

But something else happened alongside the suffering. Something that the generals did not plan for and could not fully control.

The people grew.

Across the decades of military rule, across the massacres and the silences and the children standing in the dark waiting for generals, something was accumulating in the people of Myanmar that the system had not installed and could not easily remove.

The 2021 generation was different. These were young people who had grown up during the brief democratic opening. Who had experienced press freedom, political participation, the ordinary texture of a more open society. When the coup came, they did not accept it. With a sophistication, an organisational capacity, and a moral clarity that the military had not anticipated.

What changed was the content of the moral standard itself. The older framework placed loyalty to the group above the rights of the individual. It framed suffering as karma — as personal, spiritual debt, rather than political injustice requiring political response.

The evolved framework places the dignity of every individual at the centre, regardless of ethnicity, religion, or social position. The intolerance to injustice that previous generations had been trained out of has returned. The love of freedom that the system had buried under decades of manufactured compliance has surfaced. The instinct to protect the weak has reasserted itself.

This is moral evolution. Not the kind that arrives through philosophical instruction in comfortable circumstances. The kind that is burned into a people through the experience of what its absence costs.

* * *

The World Stays Silent

And then there is the silence.

Not the silence of ignorance. The world knows. The images come through every channel. The bombed villages. The bodies in the streets. The children. The hospitals destroyed. The ordinary farmers who had nothing to do with politics and died because the military needed to demonstrate that resistance had a cost.

The world sees it. Clearly. In real time.

And the world says it is worried.

The United Nations issues statements of deep concern. The Security Council meets. China and Russia veto anything with teeth. ASEAN calls for peaceful negotiation between the people being bombed and the people doing the bombing.

Many countries went further than words. Economic sanctions were imposed. Diplomatic ties were cut or downgraded. Arms sales were prohibited. Countries voted in international bodies to isolate the military government. That is not nothing. It represents genuine political will, genuine pressure, and genuine cost to the countries that applied it.

But every mechanism with real force was blocked. China and Russia vetoed binding Security Council action. Chinese trade kept the junta economically viable while Western sanctions bit. Russian arms contracts continued. The sanctions that could have mattered were absorbed, routed around, or neutralised by the two permanent members of the Security Council who had decided the military government served their interests.

The world that tried was outweighed by the world that chose otherwise.

On social media, the desperate write.

Please help us. Please see us. Please tell someone. Please make it stop.

They write in English because English is the language of an international community that might notice. They write with photographs because photographs are harder to dismiss than words. They write with the names of the dead because names are the last dignity available to the living on behalf of those who no longer have any dignity to protect.

The world has its own chaos. Its own wars. Its own people to protect and its own calculations to make. Every nation must weigh its interests and its limits. Myanmar people understand this. It is not a grievance against the world that other countries have their own suffering to carry.

The grievance is more specific than that.

* * *

While the People Bleed, China Builds

While the people of Myanmar bleed, China builds.

This is not a conspiracy. It is not hidden. It is infrastructure. It is contracts. The Kyaukphyu deep sea port on the Bay of Bengal. Pipeline routes carrying oil and gas from the Indian Ocean directly into Yunnan province, bypassing the Strait of Malacca — the chokepoint through which eighty percent of China's energy imports currently pass and which the United States Navy could theoretically close in a conflict.

Road and rail corridors connecting the Chinese interior to the sea. Special economic zones. Contracts signed with the military government that a democratic Myanmar would have been far less willing to grant.

The logic is not complicated. China's strategic vulnerability is the Malacca Dilemma. Myanmar solves that problem. A dependent Myanmar — whose government needs Chinese protection at the UN and Chinese investment and Chinese weapons — gives China the access it needs to the Indian Ocean without the vulnerability of the Strait.

And along the border regions — the feudal arrangements that serve China's interest in managed instability. Instability enough to keep Myanmar weak and dependent. Not so much instability that it spills across the border.

The rare earth minerals being extracted at industrial scale. The people whose land it is have no meaningful say. They are not a variable in the calculation. They are the terrain.

And while this happens, the weapons flow. China and Russia supply the military government with fighter jets, artillery, and the munitions used to bomb villages and hospitals. The junta has weapons of mass destruction against a civilian population. The resistance — the people defending their country — fight with hunting rifles, improvised weapons, and equipment captured in battle. China and Russia are not neutral parties watching a conflict from a distance. They are participants. They have chosen their side with hardware and ammunition.

This is the specific injustice. Not that the world will not fight for Myanmar — Myanmar people are not asking the world to fight for them. The injustice is that powerful actors are actively ensuring the junta can continue to kill while the resistance has almost nothing to fight back with. That is not the world standing aside. That is the world tilting the scale.

> *China does not hate the people of Myanmar. It is far worse than that. It does not particularly think about them. They are an input into a calculation whose outputs are measured in strategic access, mineral extraction, and energy security.*

This is the same indifference this book has been tracing from the first chapter. Operating at the scale of a great power rather than an individual. With the resources of a continental economy rather than a single person's capacity for looking away. But the same mechanism. The same absence. The same silence where the conscience should be.

Hate is more potent than love in the calculations of great powers. Not the raw emotional hate of one person for another. The cold structural preference for self-interest over the acknowledged suffering of people who are inconveniently located at the intersection of great power competition.

Myanmar is helpless in that calculation.

Myanmar is not helpless in the knowledge of its own worth.

* * *

No One Is Coming

And also watched the world carry its own weight, as it must.

Both things are true simultaneously. The puzzle metaphor is real. And the world has other wars to fight. Holding both without letting either cancel the other is what honesty requires.

The revolution that waits for external rescue will wait forever. Not because the world is indifferent — some of it is, some of it genuinely cannot help — but because no outside force has ever been the reason a people finally won their own freedom. The conditions for freedom are built from the inside.

The revolution that survives — that plants seeds in the ground for the generation that comes after — is the one that has stopped waiting. That has understood that this is ours. That no one is coming to fight it for us. That the fight is ours, from where we stand, with what we have.

The people of Myanmar fight because they have exhausted every alternative. Because the rose has been tried and the bullet has answered. Because the saviour is not coming from outside — they are the saviour. Because the conscience, having evolved this far through this much suffering, cannot accept the terms of what the generals say is possible.

The great powers rise and fall. The logistics corridors get rerouted. The rare earth deposits get exhausted. The strategic calculations change as the circumstances that produced them change.

The conscience of a people who have decided what they are worth outlasts all of it.

The child at the roadside at five in the morning did not know that one day she or he would understand what that waiting represented. Did not know that the obedience being installed in that moment was not permanent. Did not know that suffering, honestly faced, produces something the generals cannot manufacture or confiscate.

The knowledge of what you are worth.

And the refusal — quiet, costly, ongoing, passed from one generation to the next through everything the machine can do to prevent it — to accept anyone else's answer to that question.

The moral evolution that suffering produced in the people of Myanmar is permanent. The 2021 generation grew up inside a democratic opening that no generation before them had experienced.

They know what freedom tastes like. They know the difference between the obedience that was installed in a child standing at a roadside at five in the morning, and the dignity that the conscience — once genuinely awakened — refuses to surrender.

The military can hold cities. It cannot hold that knowledge. It can imprison bodies. It cannot imprison what Aung San Suu Kyi demonstrated about what human beings are capable of when they refuse to stop being human. It can suppress the vote. It cannot suppress the generation that grew up believing the vote was theirs, and has not accepted that it was taken.

The revolution has not yet produced the political outcome it deserves. That is true, and the cost of that truth is paid in blood every day by people who did nothing to deserve it.

But the conscience of a people who have decided what they are worth — that is not a political outcome. It cannot be negotiated away or bombed into submission. It lives in the people who carry it. It is passed from one to the next. It surfaces again and again in the generation that was told to accept and refused.

No one is coming.

That is not despair. It is where belief begins. The saviour was never going to come from outside. The saviour is the person who understood that and stood up anyway. The saviour is the generation that grew up inside the fear and chose something different. The saviour is the people themselves — always was, always will be.

We are on our own.

We have always been on our own — and we have moved the line anyway.

We can do this.

We will.

Keep going.

CHAPTER NINE

Colonisation, Grief, and the Wound That Stays Open

I am not Aboriginal. I did not grow up in this country. I did not participate in its history of dispossession and I carry no ancestral claim to speak on behalf of people whose experience I cannot fully know.

I arrived carrying something else. The memory of what displacement does to a family. My great-grandparents fled China during the communist upheaval, carrying little except the willingness to start again. What they rebuilt was fragile. Later, much of that stability disappeared under political upheaval and authoritarian rule. I grew up inside the afterlife of that rupture.

When I came to Australia and learned more about Aboriginal history, I did not recognise the specifics — the land, the law, the culture, the particular cruelty of what was done here. But I recognised what it means for a people to carry loss across generations. What it means for trust to be broken at the level of a family's relationship with the state. That recognition did not come from ideology. It came from memory.

What matters now is not inherited guilt. It is honesty. The willingness to look carefully at what happened and what it is still producing. This chapter is written from that honesty — not as an expert, but as a doctor who spent six years in Alice Springs and saw what I saw.

* * *

What Was Taken

When the colonisers arrived in Australia they brought with them a framework that had no category for what they were looking at. A people whose relationship with land was legal, ceremonial, ecological, and spiritual simultaneously — a relationship that had sustained both the people and the land for at least sixty-five thousand years. The colonisers looked at it and saw nothing. Unoccupied. Available.

That belief — sincere, total, catastrophically wrong — was the ideological layer that made the dispossession possible to justify.

What was taken first was the land. Not as metaphor — as the specific, known, named, storied relationship between a people and a place. The land that was also the library. Where the knowledge of which plants healed which conditions, how the seasons moved, how the animals followed water — all of it embedded in specific locations, in ceremony, in language tied to place.

That knowledge was not primitive. It was extraordinarily sophisticated. The management of country through fire, the pharmacological knowledge of which plants healed which conditions, the ecological understanding of a continent that European science is still mapping — this was the work of sixty-five thousand years of careful attention.

When the colonisers took the land they did not only take a resource. They took the context in which the knowledge lived. The plant that grew there. The waterhole that was here. The ancestor whose story explained that place and that plant and that practice.

Severed from country, the knowledge had nowhere to live.

Then the people. The frontier violence that killed tens of thousands across the continent. Not a single event — a sustained, distributed campaign that moved with the pastoral frontier across two centuries. Conducted openly enough that it was recorded in diaries and letters and newspaper reports at the time.

* * *

The Stolen Generations

And then — the most complete form of destruction available — the children.

Between approximately 1910 and 1970, Aboriginal and Torres Strait Islander children were removed from their families by government authority. Taken to missions and institutions. Forbidden to speak their languages. Punished for practising ceremony. Trained for domestic service or manual labour. Cut off from family, country, and culture by deliberate policy.

The architects of this policy were not monsters in the dramatic sense. They believed, with complete sincerity, that they were helping. That Aboriginal culture was dying and that the kindest intervention was to remove the children before it took them down with it. The logic was paternalistic rather than cruel. And the effect was the most complete form of cultural destruction available short of outright genocide.

Remove the child from the family. Forbid the language. Punish the ceremony. Replace the identity. Cut the transmission of knowledge. Within a generation or two the culture cannot reproduce itself. The people remain but they are no longer connected to what made them who they were.

The Bringing Them Home report documented not only the immediate trauma but the multigenerational consequences. The inability to parent that follows when a person was never parented within their own culture. The loss of language that cannot be recovered when the last fluent speaker dies with no one to pass it to. Some of that knowledge is permanently gone. This needs to be said without softening. Not damaged. Not diminished. Gone.

Australia said sorry in 2008. Kevin Rudd delivered an apology that was, by most accounts, genuinely felt. The apology acknowledged the wrong. It did not address the ongoing material consequences of that wrong.

The incarceration rates. The health outcomes. The life expectancy gap. The rates of removal of Aboriginal children into child protection today — higher now, in some states, than at the height of the Stolen Generations. Saying sorry is not accountability. Accountability is what you do after saying sorry. And Australia, in most of what matters, has not done it.

What has been done instead is what this book has been calling performed virtue. The welcome to country that replaced the bilingual education program. The funding to cultural organisations that ticks a box in a government report without changing the material conditions. These performances carry some symbolic weight. Recognition matters. But recognition without resources, without structural change, without honest measurement — that is conscience salved by words while the material conditions remain unchanged.

* * *

What the Market Completed

There is something almost no one in the political conversation about Aboriginal disadvantage names plainly. The colonial project did not end with the missions and the removals. It continued through policy failures and it continues now through the market.

Introduce highly processed food and alcohol into a community of people whose physiology evolved over sixty-five thousand years on a specific diet. The metabolic response is not adaptation — it is catastrophic mismatch. The kidney failure. The cardiovascular disease. The amputation. The early death. These are not lifestyle choices. They are the predictable biological consequences of a specific food environment being introduced into a population with no evolutionary history of it.

And the alcohol. Introduced into communities that had no prior relationship with fermented beverages and therefore no cultural frameworks for managing its consumption. What has followed — the addiction rates, the liver disease, the neurological damage in children born to mothers drinking during pregnancy — is not a failure of Aboriginal willpower. It is the predictable result of introducing a powerful addictive substance into communities already destabilised by everything described above.

Australia spends significant money on closing the gap. On dialysis machines in remote communities. On hospital beds and emergency care. Very little of that investment goes upstream — to the food environment, to the alcohol supply, to the question of why these conditions exist rather than the management of what they produce. The dialysis machine treats the kidney failure the diet produced. It does not address the diet. That is not healthcare. That is the market generating the disease and the state managing its symptoms.

* * *

The People I Actually Met

In six years in Alice Springs I met people of genuine moral quality. Aboriginal people who were honest, generous, thoughtful, and deeply committed to their families and communities. Elders who knew their country with an intimacy that made my relationship with the places I had lived in seem shallow by comparison. Parents who wanted their children in school and safe and equipped for the world they would actually inhabit. Young people navigating two cultures with more grace than the situation deserved.

I also saw communities under extraordinary pressure. Violence. Addiction. Children who had absorbed the trauma of the adults around them and were expressing it outward. I am not going to pretend I did not see these things. I did. And a doctor who spent six years there and claimed to have seen only beauty would be lying.

Both things are true. Holding both without letting either one cancel the other is the beginning of the honest conversation.

A friend of mine — a nurse who came from far away to give care in one of the most difficult postings in Australian medicine — was assaulted by a patient. When I heard, my immediate question was what she had done to provoke it.

The answer is nothing. She deserved none of it. Her presence there — a nurse, caring for people, doing the work that most Australians will not do in places most Australians will not go — gave her no culpability for what was done to her. None.

The child who assaulted her is also a product of something. Not of Aboriginal culture in its original form. Of what happens to children who grow up in communities where the adults are traumatised, where alcohol has destroyed the social fabric, where violence is the language that has replaced the ones that were taken. That child is not innocent in the legal sense. And that child is also a casualty of conditions that neither my friend nor the child chose.

Both things are true. And the political conversation that contextualises the violence in ways that make it impossible to name it clearly is failing both of them. It fails my friend by treating her harm as the acceptable collateral damage of historical injustice. And it fails the child by refusing to name honestly what the conditions are producing.

When actions are presented as payback — the store broken into, the service worker harmed, the public property damaged — this is not customary law operating as designed. It is the language of customary law applied to actions the genuine customary law would not have sanctioned. The elders who hold the real law often say exactly this. Assaulting a nurse who came to give care is not justice. The ancestor whose land was taken deserves better than that as their memorial.

* * *

The Freedom Objection

When communities are asked to restrict alcohol or regulate what is sold in the local store, the objection arrives quickly. You cannot tell us what to eat. You cannot tell us what to drink. This is our freedom.

That objection deserves engagement. The history of intervention in Aboriginal communities is the history of outsiders deciding what is good for Aboriginal people and implementing it regardless of what Aboriginal people said they wanted. The missions. The welfare quarantining. The Northern Territory Intervention of 2007. That history is real and the scepticism it produces is earned.

But the freedom argument contains a confusion worth naming. A person who lives two hundred kilometres from the nearest alternative food source, who has access to one store stocking primarily processed food and soft drink — that person is not making a free choice. They are making the only available choice within a structure that has already determined what can be chosen.

In the places where communities have voted to go dry — where the decision came from within, where community members enforce it, where the evidence shows measurable improvement in child safety and school attendance — those communities are making real decisions about their own conditions. The child's freedom to grow up in safety matters more than the adult's freedom to consume what harms them.

* * *

My Daughter Is as Australian as Any Child Born Here

A patient of mine told me she was angry. Her daughter is four years old. Born in Australia. At kindergarten she is told every morning that she is a visitor in her own country.

Her anger is legitimate. Not as a rejection of what Welcome to Country is meant to do — the acknowledgment of prior ownership, the naming of ongoing dispossession. But as a response to what it has become when performed without meaning. Her daughter did not dispossess anyone. Positioning her as a visitor in the country she was born in does not address the history. It transfers its weight onto a four year old who had no part in it.

My daughter was born in Australia. She is as Australian as any child born in this country. The prior custodianship of this land by Aboriginal peoples is real and important and deserves ongoing acknowledgment. And my daughter is not a coloniser. Both of these things are true simultaneously, and any framework that cannot hold both is not doing the work it claims to be doing.

There is a version of the welcome to country that is genuinely meaningful. An acknowledgment made with real weight, that names what happened and why it still matters. That version serves the purpose it was designed for.

And there is the version that has become ritual performance. A formula recited by rote at the beginning of a conference where nothing that follows will address anything the acknowledgment named. The words spoken. Nothing changed. A conscience salved while the material conditions remain untouched.

* * *

What Accountability Actually Requires

The honest conversation eventually reaches two separate questions that are often collapsed into one.

The first: the ongoing material consequences of dispossession are real and present. The incarceration gap. The health gap. The life expectancy gap. The rates of child removal. These are not historical grievances — they are current conditions with a traceable causal relationship to historical policy. The obligation to address them does not have an expiry date. It ends when the conditions are genuinely addressed. Not when Australia announces it has addressed them. When the evidence shows it.

The second: the use of historical grievance to justify present harm to people who had no part in the history. The four year old positioned as a visitor in her own country. These things do not address the historical wrong. They redistribute its weight onto people who did not cause it.

These two things need to be separated and held separately. The first demands ongoing genuine accountability. The second demands honesty about when the form has replaced the substance. Both are compatible. Both are necessary.

Let go the grief — never, and that is right. The grief is real and some of what was lost is gone permanently. Let go the obligation to address the ongoing material consequences — not until they are addressed. Let go the use of historical grievance as justification for present harm — now, and clearly.

* * *

What I Wish For

I spent six years in Alice Springs and I cannot tell you I saw a system that worked. I saw people of genuine quality living in conditions that were failing them. I saw policy designed to help producing dependency. I saw performed virtue replacing accountability. I saw the market doing what the frontier left unfinished.

What I wish for is not complicated. It is just genuinely hard.

Good education that holds two things as non-negotiable simultaneously. The child will learn to read and write and reason and navigate the world they actually inhabit. And the child will learn their language, their country, their law, their identity. These are not competing demands. The child who knows who they are is more capable of learning, not less. The bilingual education programs that were dismantled because English-first was politically simpler were producing better literacy outcomes than the programs that replaced them. The evidence was clear. The political will to follow it was not.

A life that preserves cultural identity without being imprisoned by historical grievance. The elder who knows their country. The language alive in the mouths of children. The ceremony transmitted. The knowledge of which plants heal and which animals move where — transmitted, used, alive.

Not a museum. A living relationship between a people and the place they belong to. That is worth everything required to preserve it. And it is compatible with the child also being able to read, to govern, to participate in the broader economy of the country they inhabit.

And from the broader Australian society — genuine accountability rather than performed remorse. The upstream investment that addresses the food environment and the governance structures and the funding models rather than the downstream medicine that treats what the upstream produces. The honest conversation about what closing the gap actually requires rather than the announcement of targets that are revised every time they are missed.

My friend came from far away to give care. She deserved safety. She deserved to give care without requiring armour to do it. The child who assaulted her deserved conditions that did not produce that outcome. Building the system that delivers both is the obligation. It has not been met. It is still available to be met.

The puzzle needs every piece.

* * *

Two Cultures That Made Me

I want to say something about this country before anything else I say about it is heard as criticism.

When I arrived in Australia around ten years ago I was struggling. Looking for work. Uncertain whether I belonged. I was taken in. I did not know it at the time. I know it now.

What I found in Alice Springs surprised me. Two cultures. Both extraordinary. Both generous in ways I had not expected.

The Australian culture I encountered was something I had never seen before. Laid back in a way that initially I misread as indifference. It was not indifference. It was a quality I have come to think of as quiet dignity — the willingness to treat a person as a person without requiring them to earn it first. No performance of deference required. No elaborate hierarchy to navigate. People who would tell you something was good if it was good, and something was bad if it was bad, and who respected the same directness in return. I encountered racism in Australia, as every non-white person does. And I also encountered — far more consistently — a culture of decency that I found nowhere else in the world in quite the same form.

And then the Aboriginal patients.

The trust that built slowly and completely. The patients who brought me their artwork — bush medicine paintings, country maps in ochre and charcoal — as a form of communication that preceded and then accompanied the clinical. The way they spoke about country, about family, about connection, in a register I had no equivalent for in any of the cultures I had lived inside.

For a short time I was stationed in Mutitjulu. From the clinic window I could see Uluru. The red mountain that is also a story, a map, a law, a name for something that has no translation into English. I stood at that window many mornings and felt something I could not name. I still cannot name it adequately.

The kinship system. The sharing. The connection to country that sixty-five thousand years of continuous habitation produces. The humour — dry and immediate and completely disarming. The patience with a doctor who did not yet understand what he was looking at.

I built trust with many Aboriginal patients. Some became friends in the way that patients and doctors become friends — carefully, across the specific intimacy of illness and care. Some called me brother. I did not take that lightly. I do not take it lightly now.

There is no way that two societies this beautiful cannot find a way to live together. I refuse to believe otherwise. The grief is real. The obligation is real. The beauty on both sides is also real. And it is the beauty that I keep returning to when everything else threatens to become only its wounds.

Australia has treated me well. Better than I had any right to expect. I have a son and a daughter born here. I have colleagues who became friends and patients who taught me things no medical school could have. I have stood at a window in the centre of this continent and felt something ancient and present and completely outside the frameworks I arrived with.

I am a proud Burmese. I am a proud Australian. And I keep going — toward the day when I can say I am a proud citizen of a country that finally did what it knew it needed to do.

There must be a way. We can do it. We will.

CHAPTER TEN

The Algorithm and the Dial

Social media did not invent tribalism, outrage, or cruelty. Human beings carried those capacities long before the internet existed.

What changed was scale. And speed. And the fact that for the first time, the environment people use to form opinions about the world is designed — not to inform, but to capture attention.

The algorithm does not ask whether something is true. It asks whether you will keep looking.

* * *

What the Algorithm Does

Every major social media platform runs on the same basic logic. Attention equals revenue. The algorithm's job is to maximise time spent on the platform. And what it discovered — through billions of interactions, not through any deliberate plan — is that the content most reliably capable of holding attention is content that activates strong emotion.

Fear. Outrage. The sense that something wrong is happening and that someone should be punished for it.

These emotions are not minor. They are among the most powerful forces in human psychology. They evolved because they were useful. They activate fast and are almost impossible to reason through once triggered.

The algorithm did not create them. It discovered they are the most reliable fuel available and built a system that runs on them.

* * *

Why False Information Travels Faster

False information spreads faster, further, and to more people than true information. Not slightly faster. Significantly faster.

A study of Twitter data covering over a decade found that false news reached fifteen hundred people roughly six times faster than true information. The most viral false items concerned politics and science — the subjects where emotional stakes are highest.

The reason is not that people are foolish. Most false information is shared by ordinary people who believed it. The problem is that false information tends to be simpler and more emotionally activating than true information. True accounts include caveats, competing considerations, and uncertainty. They do not travel well.

And the correction almost never catches the original claim. By the time accurate information is available, the false version has already reached millions of people and been absorbed into existing beliefs. The belief, once formed, is hard to shift. People rarely update toward the correction. They find reasons to doubt it instead.

> *False information does not spread because people are foolish. It spreads because it was designed — consciously or not — to activate the emotions that the algorithm rewards. Truth is often complicated. Fear is always simple.*

* * *

What This Does to People

A person who is calm, unhurried, and operating inside a culture that rewards genuine reflection is capable of remarkable nuance and moral care.

A person who is anxious, constantly bombarded with emotionally activating content, and operating inside a system that rewards tribal solidarity — that person's worst capacities are being consistently amplified.

The social media environment, for most people most of the time, creates the second set of conditions. The feed is designed to generate anxiety. The notification implies something important is happening. The sense that the out-group is advancing. Anxiety is engaging. Calm is not.

What makes this hard to resist is a feature of human psychology. When calm and unhurried, we evaluate carefully — weighing evidence, considering context, updating our views. When emotionally activated and time-pressured, we fall back on faster mental shortcuts. These shortcuts are not stupid. They are ancient and often useful. But they are also systematically exploitable.

The architecture of social media is built around this. The feed moves constantly. The notification arrives before the previous item has been processed. The share button is one tap away. The design converts emotional activation into public action before the slower evaluation process has had time to operate.

Over time, the accumulated effect is a form of training. Not deliberate. But through billions of interactions inside an environment that consistently rewards speed and emotion and punishes slowness and nuance.

This is not entirely the fault of technology companies or users. The platforms respond to incentives. Users respond to emotional pressures the systems amplify. But the effect is real. A society pulled toward speed, reaction, and performance becomes less capable of the slower habits that coexistence requires — listening, sitting with uncertainty, remaining in conversation with people who see things differently.

* * *

What Is Actually Required

The honest response is not to leave. Leaving cedes the ground to the people for whom the current environment is working.

It is also not to pretend the environment is neutral. The feed has a physics. Content that activates fear and outrage moves faster than content that does not. The simple false claim travels further than the complex true one. These are not opinions. They are measurable features of how information spreads.

What is actually required is the deliberate practice of slowness inside an environment built for speed. The pause before sharing. The question asked before the reaction forms. The willingness to find the accurate version of what the opponent actually said rather than the outrage-generating version the algorithm served.

In other words — the same thing that has always been required. Letting the other person's reality be as real as your own. Practiced now in conditions specifically designed to prevent it.

Small. Unheroic. Absolutely necessary.

The feed is not the world. It only feels that way.

CHAPTER ELEVEN

Good Intentions, Poor Execution

Let me start with something that should not be controversial but has become so.

A program designed to genuinely help the vulnerable can be failing the people it was designed for. These two things are not contradictions. They can be true at the same time. And refusing to examine whether they are true — because the examination feels like an attack on the people the program was designed to help — does not protect those people. It protects the program.

* * *

The Genuine Impulse

The movement for disability rights that produced the NDIS was not manufactured. It came from decades of advocacy by people living with disability, by their families, by carers who had watched what happened when people fell outside the existing support systems. Services that dried up when funding cycles ended. People who had worked their entire lives and found in their most vulnerable moment that the system was not there.

The case for the NDIS was correct. A wealthy country should be able to guarantee that every person living with disability has access to the support they need to live with dignity and full participation in society. That guarantee should not depend on geography or the lottery of which funding round happened to be open.

That is a genuine moral commitment. The people who fought for it were right to fight for it. What follows is not an argument against that commitment. It is an argument about what happened to it.

* * *

What the Numbers Show

When the NDIS was designed, the Productivity Commission's 2010 estimate put the annual cost at around fifteen billion dollars. By 2024-25, according to the Australian Government's 2025-26 Budget, it was spending close to fifty billion dollars annually. According to the NDIS Annual Pricing Review Report, by 2021-22 the scheme had already outstripped Medicare in total federal expenditure. The per-participant comparison makes this even starker. Medicare serves the entire Australian population of over twenty-seven million people; the NDIS serves around six hundred and fifty thousand participants. According to NDIA data, the average annual plan value is around sixty-six thousand dollars per participant — against roughly seventeen hundred dollars per Medicare patient. The per-person investment the NDIS makes is extraordinary by any measure — which reflects the genuine severity of need it was designed to address. It also means the question of whether that investment is reaching the right people in the right way deserves honest scrutiny.

The growth is not straightforwardly explained by more people receiving more support. Average plan sizes have grown substantially. The provider market has expanded and prices have risen. Administrative costs were consistently underestimated. There are widely reported concerns about provider integrity — billing practices that regulators and auditors have flagged as requiring tighter oversight.

This needs to be said carefully. The vast majority of the people working inside this system — the support workers, the carers, the coordinators, the therapists — are people doing genuinely difficult and often underpaid work because they care about the people they support. There are thousands of them. Many have given years of their lives to this work. The critique here is of the system design and the incentive structures it created, not of the people doing the work honestly inside it. The problem is not the workers. The problem is that the system has also attracted, in some cases, providers whose interests are not the participant's — and it has not been well designed to distinguish between them.

The scheme's participant numbers grew substantially beyond initial projections. Some of this reflects genuine unmet need finally being identified — the scheme reached people who had never had adequate support before. Some reflects a broader definition of disability than original modelling assumed. Reforms passed in 2024 tightened eligibility criteria and aimed to redirect some foundational supports to state-funded services, bringing the growth rate down from over twenty percent to around ten percent.

The question is not whether people with genuine disability deserve support. They unambiguously do. The question is whether the scheme is directing its resources toward the people who need it most — or whether its growth reflects incentive structures the original designers did not adequately anticipate.

The people who need the scheme most — those with the most complex and significant disabilities — report mixed experiences. Some describe genuine transformation. Others describe a system so complex to navigate, so consumed by review and paperwork, that the energy required to access the support leaves little energy for the life it was supposed to enable.

* * *

To Check a Man Doing His Job, You Create a Job for a Man to Check Only

Every system begins with a genuine idea. And the logic of institutional self-preservation gets inside that idea and begins, slowly, to redirect it.

A program is announced. Money flows. Some is not used as intended. A scandal emerges. The response is oversight — new rules, new reporting requirements, new auditing processes, new positions to monitor compliance. The people in those positions are doing a legitimate job. The rules they enforce are there because real abuses occurred.

To check a man doing his job, you create a job for a man to check only.

And then you check the checker.

And their salaries, their offices, their systems — all of this comes from the same pool of money that was supposed to reach the person who needed a support worker three afternoons a week.

What is harder to find than the total cost of the scheme is a clear public accounting of what proportion reaches the intended beneficiary versus what is consumed by the system built to deliver it. A system confident that its resources were reaching their intended destination would have reason to make that ratio visible. The difficulty of finding it is itself part of the story.

* * *

The Silence of the Vulnerable

Every market requires informed consumers who can evaluate providers, report poor service, and walk away from arrangements that do not serve them. This discipline keeps markets honest.

The NDIS created a market for disability support services. And many of the people that market was created to serve are among the least equipped to function as the informed consumers a well-functioning market requires. The person with severe cognitive disability who cannot evaluate whether the service represents value. The person with complex communication needs who cannot easily report that the provider charged for hours not worked. The person in acute mental health crisis who is in no position to navigate a dispute resolution process.

These are not edge cases. They are the people the scheme was designed for. And they are precisely the people whose silence makes them the easiest targets when oversight is insufficient.

It is not an attack on people with disability to say that the system designed to support them has developed structural problems that deserve honest examination. It is the strongest possible argument for fixing the system. The people the scheme was designed to help deserve one that works.

* * *

When Protecting the Goal Prevents Fixing the System

There is a specific dynamic worth naming precisely. The political conversation around programs designed to help the vulnerable has developed a structure in which any criticism of the program's execution can be framed as hostility toward its beneficiaries.

That framing is politically powerful. It is also, in most cases, dishonest. And it produces, systematically, the outcome it claims to prevent.

When the honest observation — this program has grown well beyond initial projections and there are widely reported concerns that the additional cost is not proportionally reaching the people it was designed to help — cannot be made without being interpreted as an attack on people with disability, the program cannot be reformed.

The political environment that makes it difficult to examine a program's efficiency is not protecting the vulnerable. It is preventing the reforms that would make the program genuinely serve them better.

The same logic applies in every domain. Universal healthcare is good — and specific implementations at specific times may produce outcomes that deserve honest examination without that examination constituting an argument against healthcare. The distinction between the impulse and the execution is one that genuine supporters of the impulse have to be willing to make. Because the alternative is to protect a failing execution in the name of an impulse that the execution is betraying.

* * *

What Is Actually Required

I think of the people I saw in Alice Springs. People with genuine disability, genuine need, genuine courage in conditions that would have broken many of us. They did not need a performance of support.

They needed the support worker to actually show up.

The plan to actually make sense. The funding to actually reach them rather than the organisation billing for their name. What they deserved was not complicated. What they received was, too often, a system working hard to serve itself.

What is required is the willingness to say this without being accused of opposing the support. It requires the person who believes in supporting the vulnerable to examine honestly whether the specific system is doing that. It requires the politician who announced the program to ask whether it is producing what it promised. It requires the provider doing genuine work to name and report the providers who are not.

The system is not the purpose. It was built to serve the purpose. When it begins to consume the purpose it was built to serve, the honest response is to return to that purpose.

That insistence will generate accusation from people who have confused the system with the purpose. That accusation is worth bearing.

Because the alternative — protecting the system in the name of the purpose while it fails the people the purpose was supposed to serve — is not compassion.

It is, once again, the performance of compassion.

And the people whose lives depend on the system being genuine rather than performed cannot afford the performance.

CHAPTER TWELVE

The Transaction

Politics is supposed to be the mechanism through which a society decides what it values and what it is willing to build together. At its best that is what it is. At its most degraded it becomes something simpler — the exchange of benefits for votes, managed on a four-year cycle.

This chapter is not an argument against democracy. It is an argument for it — for what it is supposed to be rather than what it has become in too many of its current expressions.

* * *

The Transaction

The logic is simple enough to state plainly. A politician who wants to win an election identifies a group whose votes they need. They offer that group something — a payment, a benefit, a policy that serves their immediate interests. The group votes accordingly. The transaction is complete.

The thing offered is often genuinely good. Welfare payments may genuinely need to increase. Housing assistance is genuinely needed. Disability support is genuinely necessary. The problem is not the thing offered. The problem is the question being asked when it is offered.

A government doing its job properly asks: what does this society need, and what is the most efficient and equitable way to provide it? The cost to the public should be proportional to the genuine benefit. The timing should reflect genuine need. The design should reflect careful analysis of what actually works.

A government conducting a transaction asks something different: what does this group need to vote for me, and can I offer it before election day?

These are not the same question. And the answer to the second question produces something different from the answer to the first. The welfare payment calibrated not to genuine need but to electoral timing.

The benefit designed not for maximum impact but for maximum visibility to the target constituency. The announcement made before the election, the review scheduled after it.

The people who receive the benefit are not wrong to take it. They are responding rationally to what is being offered. The problem is not the voter. The problem is the politician who designed the transaction and the system that permits it.

Over time the transaction corrupts the purpose of government from the inside. Not dramatically. Gradually. Each individual decision locally rational — this group needs this, they will vote for us if we provide it — produces, in aggregate, a government whose primary skill is distributing benefits to the groups whose votes it needs rather than solving the problems the society actually faces.

The problems that require sacrifice, complexity, and time horizons longer than the next election — these are the ones that transactional politics cannot address. They do not produce visible benefits before polling day. They require asking people to accept a cost now for a gain they will not see for twenty years.

They require making someone worse off in order to make the whole better.

No transaction is designed around those problems. Transactions are designed around the problems that can be solved by spending money on people who vote.

* * *

Divide and Conquer

The transaction requires funding. And funding requires taxation. Which creates a second political problem — the group being taxed to fund the handout is unlikely to be enthusiastic about it.

The solution is division. If the group receiving the handout and the group funding it are busy resenting each other, neither of them is looking at the arrangement clearly. Old versus young. Local versus immigrant. Those who own property versus those who cannot afford it. Those on welfare versus those who pay for it.

These divisions are real. The tensions between them are genuine. The resentment on each side is not manufactured from nothing. But the political use of them is deliberate — to keep the groups who are actually paying for the system focused on each other rather than on who is actually benefiting from it.

Because the people who fund political parties are not the everyday Australians in these groups. They are the gas companies, the property developers, the industry lobbies, the organisations with enough money to make political donations matter. These donors receive their return quietly — a regulation softened, a subsidy extended, a tax arrangement that ordinary accountants cannot access. Not a handout announced at a press conference. A favour delivered without press conference at all.

The ordinary Australian — whether they arrived last year or have been here for generations, whether they are twenty-five or seventy — is not the political donor. They are the revenue source and the audience for the theatre that keeps them from noticing where the money actually goes.

This is the full transaction. Not just the handout to the voter. The handout to the voter, funded by the tax on the other voter, managed through a division that keeps both groups occupied with each other, while the genuine beneficiaries of the political relationship collect their return quietly in the background.

It is not a conspiracy. It does not require anyone to sit in a room and plan it. It is the predictable outcome of a system where political funding comes from organised money and political support comes from organised groups, and the politician's job is to satisfy both without either noticing the full cost of the arrangement.

* * *

Migration and Politics

Migration is where the transaction is most visible because it offers two tools simultaneously. A party that positions itself as welcoming to a specific immigrant community creates a loyal voting bloc — the migrant who arrived under that party's policies has a reason to vote for them that has nothing to do with the party's broader fitness to govern.

The mirror image is equally available. A party that positions itself against immigration tells the economically anxious that the outsider is the explanation for their situation. Neither tool requires the politician to actually think about what immigration policy should produce — what genuine integration requires, what the country can absorb well, what conditions benefit both those arriving and those already there.

The migrant is not a policy question in either case. They are a vote calculation. And both calculations share the same essential disrespect — converting the human being into an instrument of electoral strategy.

The person who migrates deserves honest engagement. Not calculation. Not blame. They made one of the most consequential decisions a human being can make — to leave the place that shaped them and build a life somewhere new. That decision deserves to be treated as what it is.

* * *

What the Debate Has Become

The political debate — designed to let citizens evaluate the people who want to lead them — has in many democracies stopped resembling its stated purpose.

It is a performance of dominance. Who interrupts more effectively. Who delivers the better line. Who projects certainty regardless of whether the certainty is warranted.

By the time fact-checkers publish their assessments the debate has reached its audience and impressions have formed. The correction arrives after the claim has spread. And the voter trying to extract genuine information about what will actually happen to their healthcare, their wages, their children's future — is watching the wrong show.

The show is not designed to inform. It is designed to perform strength to the base. The base does not want information. It wants confirmation.

* * *

What Mandatory Voting Does

Australia's system of mandatory voting changes the political culture in ways worth understanding.

In systems where voting is optional, parties focus their energy on turning out their base. Politics increasingly speaks to the already-convinced. Policy is designed to energise the committed rather than speak to the undecided.

When everyone votes, that calculation changes. Politicians cannot win by simply activating their base. They must speak to ordinary people who are not partisan, who hold mixed views, who are trying to make a reasonable judgment.

That does not guarantee wisdom. But it does mean a politics that has to reach ordinary people is at least required to make some contact with ordinary life — and that is different from a politics that only needs to satisfy its most committed supporters.

Democracy is not valuable because it produces perfect outcomes. It is valuable because it allows disagreement without requiring enemies. It allows the society to change direction without violence.

* * *

The Honest Answer

A colleague once said to me — your country needs a lot of things. Maybe it is that way because you all migrated. Maybe you should go back.

I did not say what I was thinking. I thought about it for a long time afterward.

My honest answer — the one I have never been fully comfortable saying out loud — is this.

I left because I am a selfish coward. Who put myself, my family, and my future generation's interest above my country.

Am I bad? Yes. The dial is that I am a selfish person for the people I love.

I put my children's future above the future of the country that made me. I chose the free and empathic environment over the one that needed me. I support the resistance from the other side of the world in the ways available to me. But I am not there. They are.

I do not dress this in the language of nobility. I left because I wanted my children to grow up free. That is a self-interested reason. It is also the most human reason available. And the honesty this book has been arguing for — the kind that does not let you escape into comfortable stories about yourself — will not let me call it anything else.

What I can say is this. I contribute. I work. I stay honest. I carry Myanmar in everything I do and I try to make the country that took me in proud of the choice it made.

The dial moves in both directions. The selfish coward who loves his children is also the doctor who showed up. Who was called brother. Who stood in a clinic in Mutitjulu with Uluru in the window and understood that this country was worth everything it asked of him.

That is my relationship to Australia. Not the performance of gratitude. The real thing. The kind that includes the honest account of why I came and what it cost and what I chose and what I still owe.

* * *

I came from a country where the military took power because it could. Where the democratic opening was brief and genuine and was ended by men with guns who decided that the will of the people was an inconvenience.

I look at the democracies that remain intact and I see something extraordinary that is easy to take for granted from the inside. The ability to disagree without becoming enemies. The ability to change direction without violence. The ability to hold power accountable without disappearing in the night.

These things are not automatic. They require maintenance from everyone inside the system. From politicians who choose the long view over the transaction. From voters who ask what does this country need rather than what does this party offer me.

And from the migrants who chose this — who left a place where the genuine article was unavailable and came to a place where it exists, imperfectly, precariously, requiring constant attention from the people inside it.

We have perhaps the clearest view of what is at stake. We have seen what the alternative looks like. We have lived inside it.

We chose this instead. Not the performance of democracy. The real thing.

The vote is not a transaction. It is a responsibility. The politician is not a vendor offering the best deal. They are a steward of the public trust.

The question, in every moment, is whether enough people are willing to demand that.

A Final Word — What Now

What This Book Is Saying

This book did not set out to solve anything. It set out to be honest about what human beings are, what we do with the institutions we build, and what it costs — and what it takes — to keep the conscience alive inside systems that consistently reward looking away.

The conscience came first. Before the religion that tried to codify it. Before the political system that tried to institutionalise it. Before the ideology that tried to claim it. The basic sensitivity to another person's reality — the recognition that their suffering is as real as yours — precedes every system that has ever tried to own it.

The choice is always available. Not heroism. Not the dramatic gesture. The specific, ordinary, available thing — from where you stand, with what you have, in this moment.

Perhaps we are all pieces of a puzzle. That sentence, spoken by a colleague in Myanmar to a doctor who needed to hear it, has stayed with me. Not through the heroic individual who changes everything. Through the accumulation of specific people, in specific moments, each contributing the thing that only their position makes possible. All pieces. All necessary. None sufficient alone.

That weight is already present. The moral sense keeps appearing — in the generation that marched when the previous accepted the silence, in the elder who kept the language alive until there was someone to receive it. The weight of all those moments is the only force that has ever actually moved the line. Not quickly. Not safely. But moved it.

* * *

From Where I Stand

I left Myanmar. I built a life in a country that gave me more than I had any right to expect. And I have watched that freedom. On the transaction. On the algorithm. On the performed concern that costs nothing and changes nothing.

I do not say this with contempt. I say it with the specific concern of someone who has seen the alternative. Who knows what the absence of a functioning democracy looks like. Who grew up inside the fear of a state that had decided the conscience was dangerous.

The genuine article is worth fighting for. Not because it is perfect. Because it is the best arrangement human beings have produced for protecting the conscience from the concentration of power. And it is fragile. Not from external enemies. From the internal drift toward comfort and transaction and the slow replacement of moral engagement with its performance.

The correction requires people who are willing to make it. That is all. That is everything.

* * *

The World We Hand Forward

Every generation inherits a partially broken world. We inherit systems shaped by previous fears, previous ambitions, previous acts of courage and previous acts of cowardice. Then we add our own layer to the inheritance.

The question is not whether we will build a perfect world. We will not. The question is whether we leave the next generation slightly more humane systems, slightly stronger truth, slightly deeper compassion, slightly less fear, than the ones we inherited ourselves.

That difference matters enormously across centuries.

* * *

Myanmar

Part of me still lives emotionally in Myanmar.

In the people still resisting fear there. In the grief of watching a country repeatedly trapped between hope and violence. In the guilt many migrants carry after building safety elsewhere while others remain inside danger.

But Myanmar also taught me something I cannot forget.

Human dignity survives conditions that should destroy it completely.

Students protesting despite bullets. Doctors treating patients despite arrest. Ordinary civilians helping one another despite enormous risk.

The systems surrounding human beings matter profoundly. But something inside people still resists total domination — repeatedly, throughout history, against the odds.

That resistance may be fragile.

It is also real.

* * *

Coexistence

The older I become, the less interested I am in victory narratives.

The world is too interconnected, too psychologically fragile, and too dangerous for endless tribal triumphalism. No civilisation survives permanently through humiliation alone. No society remains healthy when entire groups stop recognising one another's humanity.

Coexistence is not weakness.

It is maturity. Not agreement on everything. Not moral relativism. Not pretending serious conflicts disappear. Simply the recognition that human beings sharing one planet must eventually learn how to disagree without permanently dehumanising one another.

* * *

Hope

I said at the beginning this is not an optimistic book in the simple sense.

Too much suffering exists for easy optimism. But hopelessness is also a form of surrender. And history does not justify complete hopelessness.

Human beings repeatedly surprised history. Abolishing systems once considered permanent. Expanding rights once unimaginable. Rebuilding after devastation. Producing solidarity across divisions that once appeared absolute.

Progress is uneven. Reversible. Incomplete. But possible.

Hope may not be confidence that everything will improve automatically. Perhaps hope is simply the refusal to stop acting as though conscience matters — even when history becomes discouraging.

* * *

The Light

The title of this book came from a feeling I have struggled to describe properly. Let me try now.

Think of a room that has been closed against the light. The windows boarded. The curtains drawn. Every gap sealed against the intrusion of something the people inside have decided they do not want to see.

And then think of dawn.

Dawn does not negotiate. It does not ask permission. It does not give up because the window was blocked yesterday. It comes back the next morning and tries again — through the crack in the boards, the gap at the edge of the curtain, the small hole that was overlooked. Persistent. Indifferent to resistance. Returning on a schedule that nothing human has ever successfully interrupted for long.

That is what conscience is.

Not the dramatic gesture. Not the hero arriving. Just the light that keeps returning to the room that tried to shut it out. Finding the crack. Entering anyway. A little at a time. Until the person inside cannot pretend they did not see it.

Propaganda tries to board the windows. Fear draws the curtains. Tribalism and ideology and the comfort of not having to think too hard — these are the materials people use to keep the light out. And sometimes they work, for a while, for a generation, in a country, in an institution, in a person.

But not permanently.

The light comes back.

We already have what it takes to receive it. The sensitivity is built in — the recognition of another person's suffering, the recoil at cruelty, the knowledge of what dignity looks like and what its absence looks like. We were born with it before any doctrine arrived to name it.

We do not need to manufacture conscience.

We only need to stop blocking the window.

The light keeps returning.

Through the crack. Through the gap left open. Through the part of us that still recognises another human being when we see them suffering.

Let it in.

www.ingramcontent.com/pod-product-compliance
Lightning Source LLC
LaVergne TN
LVHW091146080826
845145LV00008B/2271

* 9 7 8 1 7 6 4 6 9 0 9 0 4 *